Once Round the Umbrella Tree

Once Round
the Umbrella Tree

by

ELSIE GADSBY

BBC Radio Derby and
Derbyshire Library Service

A joint publishing venture by
BBC Radio Derby, St Helens Street
Derby DE1 3HY and
Derbyshire Library Service

Designed and produced by
Ashgrove Press Ltd
Bath BA1 2PD
Printed in Great Britain

To John
for forty wonderful years

Chapter One

It was brimstone and treacle time again. A few days after my birthday in March, Spring would make its welcome appearance. That was the sign for all the women around us to go mad. Carpets (for those who could afford them) were taken outside and slung over clothes lines, and the accumulation of a year's dust and grime banged out of them, usually with a walking stick, or with a carpet beater for those fortunates who could afford one. There were no vacuum cleaners at that period, 1927; most cleaning being done with soft and hard hand-brushes, and a sweeping brush.

Whitewash, emulsion paint as we know it, would be slapped on the ceilings and new wallpaper chosen for the walls. Of course, being so hard up we couldn't afford to have the living room papered every year. Once every four or five years was the norm for us.

But Dad always whitewashed the outside lavatory and washhouse every year. He wasn't very skilled at the job and there'd be runs of the stuff forming weird patterns on the inside doors. Yes - he whitewashed the woodwork as well. I remember one day he'd spent rather a long time in the lav, and Mam wondered if he was alright. He came in just then.

"I've done a picture," he told us. "A lovely row of trees and a river."

"Where Dad?" I asked.

"On the closet door," he informed us. "I did it wi' the burnt edge of me'match." He'd been sitting there on the long wooden seat over the pan, leaning forward to trace around the lines made by the runs of whitewash. Sure enough, as I found later when the fugg of tobacco smoke had cleared and I dared venture into the lav, there was a pattern of tall trees and a stream etched on the back of the door.

"Yer've made a right mess o' that," our Mam told him. "Yer'll have to whitewash over it agen'."

"NEVER." He was most indignant. "You don't appreciate my artistic talents." I did, but I kept quiet, tact being a virtue I was fast acquiring with my approaching adolescence.

But back to the brimstone and treacle. At the first breath of Spring Mam would send me across the road to Buick Sissons. He had open-topped corn bins and maize bins along one wall. There were so many people who kept fowls, Buick's corn was a God-send to them.

On the wall behind his counter was a green treacle barrel, with a handle sticking out in front.

"Two pennorth of treacle please," I would ask, and Buick would place my jam jar on the shelf under the barrel and out would flow the dark brown, sticky substance. I would hold my breath until the handle was fully turned again, stopping the flow. I secretly longed for the handle to stick, so that the treacle would run down among the blocks of snow white salt stacked below.

"Here yar' me gel. Brimstone and treacle time agen' is it?" he would say. He was a bonny man with gingery hair and bushy moustache, a well-known figure in the Cotmanhay area, as were his wife and well-dressed daughters. Mrs. Sisson was slim, dark-haired and looked and dressed like a duchess, with her small toque hats, and the veiling swathed around her face.

Back home Mam would mix flowers of sulphur with the treacle, and systematically dose each of us with it in turn. This ritual went on for about a month, or until she'd decided we'd had a really good 'clear out'. I usually felt as though I'd lost my bowels in the process, as well as my spots and pimples, and visits to the lav were timed so that I would not immediately follow another member of the family. There were no Air Fresheners to sprinkle around in those days.

By this time I'd started work at the factory, as a silk winder, a job I detested at first but grew to tolerate as I became more experienced. Besides, I was now handing Mam five shillings wage every week, and getting back sixpence pocket money. Now in 1927 sixpence or ninepence pocket money was considered adequate for a school-leaver. How to spend it was the problem.

I was becoming increasingly hair conscious. I still wore my hair in plaits, and on Saturday nights Mam still wound my hair in rag strips, producing tight ringlets on Sunday but bushy curls by Monday, when I'd combed out the ringlets.

I started to buy shampoos, and managed to make one packet last for three weeks. The shampoo made my hair shine, and it smelt gorgeous.

Edie and Leshia, the two young women I worked with in the winding room, used a little booklet of Carmine leaves to colour their cheeks and lips. They'd detach a leaf, moisten it with spittle and dab away at their cheeks and lips. The result looked clownish if not applied properly, as I soon discovered when I first tried it out in a secluded corner of the winding room.

"Yer' want a bit more spit on yer' fingers," Leshia told me.

Well, I got some right funny looks from the foreman and his lad, when I went through the warping room on my way to the stairs, and when I got home Mam took one look and snapped.

"What's that muck yer've got one yer' face? Yer' not old enough yet fer' me'kup; yer' can goo' an wash it off."

So - after that I'd wipe my carmined cheeks and lips with saliva on a bit of rag I kept in my pocket for that purpose - before I got in the house.

I never got the boiled ham or soft-boiled egg I'd always yearned for, for my tea. It was always dripping or jam, or cold, stewed rhubarb and custard. So - I gave up my longing and ate what was on the table.

After I'd been at the factory for a fortnight, I asked Mam if I could have an extra three-pence a week pocket money, making it up to a shilling. I thought she was going to explode.

"Yer' all alike, soon as yer' start work yer' wantin' all yer' money on yer' back," she grumbled.

"But I don't want it for clothes Ma," I protested, "I want to be able to go to the pictures in the week."

"Yer'd better ask for a rise at work then. Then yer' can have more pocket money."

Now at that tender age, factory bosses were on an equal with Prime Ministers, Police Superintendants and Bishops in my estimation. I'd never dare ask for a rise. But I knew I'd have to if I was to have more pocket money, so I decided I'd try my luck, if I could pluck up enough courage to approach the big boss on Friday, pay day.

General Store

When I got up that morning I had diarrhoea, and I couldn't eat much breakfast. I seemed to be running to the lav all day, and when I nipped home at dinner time, Mam gave me some nutmeg grated in milk.

"Don't forget to ask fer' that rise," was her parting shot, making my tummy do another somersault.

Pay time crawled round slowly that day, and by the time my turn came my lips were dry with so much licking, and my innards were doing strange things.

"Please Sir - her - Mam says I ought to have a rise." I managed to squeeze the words out of my tight lips. I waited for the big boss to explode. But he merely smiled.

"Oh she did did she? Well," a long pause whilst he surveyed me quizzically, "We shall have to see about it then. I'll see what Mr. Granger says about your work." Mr. Granger was the foreman-cum-warper.

But the next weekend there was an extra halfcrown in my pay packet. That pleased our Mam and she gave me a few coppers extra pocket money. Now I'd be able to go to the pictures in the week. I still went occasionally with my brother Dan on Saturday afternoons, but I felt I was getting too big now to get in for a penny. Besides, I was getting some curious looks from the cashier, for I was tall for a fourteen year old.

So, the week following my pay rise I started to go to the pictures one night in the week, on my own. I used to walk the mile and a half up the town and back. I didn't want to waste money going on the tram. Besides, the streets were a lot safer then than they are now; no fear of rapes or muggings.

One night I went to see a Greta Garbo film. She was a great favourite of mine, beautiful but so aloof. I used to envy her quiet composure. I sat on a row of empty seats half way down. It only cost fourpence halfpenny at this lower half. I was vaguely aware of someone moving into the seat next to me. But it wasn't long before I was also aware of his furtive movements, his hand slowly moving towards my knee. I was terrified, panic-stricken, wondering what to do. I was still innocent at fourteen, naive, not fully realising the danger I was in, but sufficiently aware that this should not be happening. Then, with unbelievable courage I was on my feet and moving rapidly along the row. I searched in the semi-darkness until I found a seat between two elderly women. But the rest of the evening was spoiled for me, and I was still trembling as I walked home.

Next day, on my way to work I mentioned the incident to one of my old school pals who'd started work at a nearby factory. She'd left school a year before me, but was very much a loner.

"Ya' want to do same as I do," she told me. "Stick a hatpin under ya' coat lapel, an' then if any on' em' starts 'owt, let 'em have it - right through their hand. They don't like that."

I looked at her with awe - tinged I might add with a great respect. But I was able to put her advice to the test the following week. I again went in the fourpenny-ha'pennies at the King's Picture house. A Hamburger Bar stands there now, where once was the imposing white front facade.

The usual dirty mac slouchers were lounging over the back seats, searching for their prey. I chose an end, empty seat, ready for a quick getaway. It wasn't long before someone crept into the seat beside me, and started the now familiar slow hand grope. I put my hand to my coat rever where reposed one of Mam's large hatpins. Hlding my breath I made a sharp, stabbing downward movement. You should have heard the yell he let out, and the curses as he quickly retreated along the row, before the Cinema manager came to see what all the fuss was about. But I was left in peace after that to enjoy the film, and you can be sure from then on I never went to the pictures without my hatpin.

Chapter Two

I soon got used to factory life, and began to enjoy my silk winding job. Fortunately I was an adaptable person. But always at the back of my mind was the feeling that life had somehow cheated me.

I'd have made a great nurse, something I'd dreamed of doing over the last few years, but, as Mam had said,

"There's no bl . . . . money in nursing me' gel."

And of course I'd have done marvellous at Art School, but where would the money have come from? Certainly not from my collier Dad. Whoever heard of a collier's kid becoming a great artist? And so the seeds of frustration were sown, and on what a fertile soil, for I was a sensitive creature and filled with a lively imagination.

When my swifts were all spinning, and the bobbins of synthetic silk slowly filling, I would go off into my own private dream world. Sometimes I'd be walking softly along a ward between the snowy white beds, pausing to lay my soft hand on a fevered brow, or lifting a cup to some dry, aged lips. And then I'd be filled with a deep sense of peace.

Then I'd go off at random, surrounded by sketches and swathes of material, about to embark on one of my artistic creations, for my Art education would have taken a practical turn, and I would try my hand at dress designing. But I'd come down to earth with a bang.

"Eh up you - wake up - yer've got some ends broke," one of the young women would call to me. Then would come that sick feeling of frustration, and I'd have to bite my lip to keep back a sharp retort.

When the Spring merged into Summer I began to feel

stifled, for the windows along the south side of the factory, catching all the sun, made the place like a greenhouse, and I'd stand on the hot water pipes (cold now), and gaze longingly over the fields towards Cossall, and the dumpy church tower among the trees, and away to far distant Strelley.

This view looked so gloriously inviting, and I'd feel choked with longing for the fresh air, and green space around me, for I was a true child of nature. But I made up for it in the evenings and the weekends; that is if Mam didn't want me to take the baby out.

The baby, Marian, was now three years old, but still regarded as a baby by us all. She was pretty as a new doll, pale skin, pink cheeks, and long lashes shading her grey eyes. Mam would put her in the wooden, canvas bottomed push-chair, wrap a piece of grey blanket around her, tightly tucking in the ends, and I'd push her along for miles.

"Look at the pretty flowers – Ooh, what a lovely butterfly." Then I'd point to a trail of smoke in the distance, "A puff train. What is it Marie?" using my pet name for her.

She would look around her solemnly. "Train" she would say.

But mostly I'd meet my particular friend of the moment, Elsie Middleton. She had a thick mane of ginger hair, a lovely wide grin and marvellous white teeth. She'd bring along her shaggy mongrel dog and we'd go for long walks across the fields. Elsie could vault over five barred gates like a tomboy, but when I tried it I ricked my back, so had to be content with the stile or squeeze-through.

Elsie was thin and freckle-faced, friendly and loyal. A true gem of a pal. So it was no surprise when she told me a boy named Cyril had asked her to be his girl friend.

"I can tell him No, if you like," she said. She was like that, as I said, loyal.

"No – you go with him," I told her, but felt a great sense of loss and learned one of the greatest lessons in life. Nothing goes on forever.

Cossall·Church Tower

It was during that Summer when airplane rides were advertised on placards around the town, and by the town crier. The venue was to be a large field beside the Shipley Boat Inn at the bottom of Long Lane. The flights were to cost a few shillings, and there was great speculation as to who would be the first intrepid soul with enough money, and guts, to climb into this double winged, wobbly looking contraption.

There we were, hundreds of kids and their Mams and Dads, holding the littlest ones aloft, the better to see this new phenomenon, all peering over the hedge, for we were not allowed on the actual flight field. Someone climbed into the passenger seat, people cheered, the plane wobbled slightly as it moved forward.

"Look at that our Else," Mam was pointing excitedly. But I was looking at something else – mouth agape. I'd never seen anything like this before. Oh I'd heard about it, at the factory.

"What ya' lookin' at?" Mam wanted to know. I pointed. A woman was standing a few feet away. She wore no hat, which was unusual in itself, but her black straight hair was cut short, with a fringe over her forehead. She had BOBBED HAIR, the first I had ever seen.

"What a funny looking woman," our Dan said when I nudged him to have a look. Dan was a bit younger than me. Harold was there too. He was six years old and had eyes only for the plane.

All the other women still wore their hair in a bun at the back of their heads, hats pushed forward slightly, and a frizz of hair at the side of their cheeks. But it was not long after that before other women followed suit, and I among them. As Mam used to say, "Ya' might as well be outa' the world as outa' fashion." This was always one of her pet phrases. So she too had her hair bobbed; but ever after that it was I who trimmed it for her, using our one and only pair of scissors. They were used for trimming bacon rinds, cutting toe nails, cutting wall paper, trimming the hairs sprouting from Dad's nostrils, and a hundred other things. Our Dad said:

"Yer've made a good job o' that gel; better cut mine annal."
And so that was another job I acquired over the years.

But the thing I found difficult was trying to cut my own hair
at the back, perched on the edge of Mam's dressing table and
with another mirror held at an angle so's I could see the back
of my head. Many's the time I nicked my ear lobe, but I
couldn't afford to go to the newly opened hairdresser's shop.

We had one week's holiday in August, when the whole
factory closed down. There were no paid holidays for the
workers at that time, so Mam had to put a bit by each week to
cover the holiday period. I still expected to get my pocket
money, and I must have totally ignored the fact that I still
needed to be fed.

Some families went to the seaside for that week; Skeggie
mostly - the more careful people who had saved a little money
each week throughout the year. They were mostly the families
of fathers who did not drink or smoke so much - as Dad
anyway.

No such luck for us. Our outings were a walk down
Skevington's Lane and across the fields to the Shipley Boat for
a bottle of lemonade for us kids, shared of course, and a few

Shipley Boat Inn

pints for Dad and a glass of beer for our Mam. But we'd have a bag of monkey nuts (peanuts), and these we would share as we walked along.

I always kept two of the longest, nipped open the ends and clipped them on to my ear lobes, dangling like earrings. All the girls used to do this. A sign of vanity? I wonder. I was growing up fast.

But on this holiday week Mam and Dad took us to Matlock Bath for the day. We got on the train at the branch line station at the bottom of Bath Street, where the Trent Garage now stands. When we arrived at the Junction at Cossall we changed trains, and got on to the line which took us through Langley Mill, Ambnergate, Cromford where the wooded hills started, and on to Matlock Bath.

We walked beside the river, we clambered up the steep narrow roadway to Abraham Heights, and saw the breathtaking views across to Riber Castle. We marvelled at the petrifying wells and the large goldfish in the pond beside the Pavilion; and we ate our picnic tea in the River Gardens.

It was the first time I'd ever been in the Matlock region, but what a lasting impression those rocks and heights had on me – and the sound of the rushing river was like music in my ears. I'd been transported to heaven for a day.

At that time it was no strange sight to see Mothers and Fathers with six or seven kids, yes teenagers among them, taking their Sunday evening walk. Often the man would be striding along in front, chest stuck out like a cock pheasant, with Mother behind pushing the pram or push chair, a kid hanging on to each handle, and the older children dawdling behind, no doubt wishing they could have been with pals of their own age.

I began to feel this urge to want to break away from parental influence at a very much later date, but for the present I felt more secure to be in the bosom of my family.

Chapter Three

October came round and it was time for our annual Fair. This was the first time I'd not gone around it with my brother Dan. I'd arranged to go with some of my old school pals who were now all at work. None of the rides cost above a penny or twopence, and seemed to last much longer than they do now. The cake-walk was my favourite. I didn't care for the helter-skelter - too childish I thought; and I loathed the huge twin steamboats. I liked to walk around and eat nougat or brandysnap. I'm quite certain there were no hot-dog stalls at that time, I can't remember any. But there were the cockles and whelks stalls, and the mushy peas which did a roaring trade, as did the long, colourful stalls which sold brandy snap, gingerbread and Grantham biscuits and pink and white squares of nougat. And every toffee stall had it's cocks on sticks, a highly coloured confection which vied in popularity with the ever faithful toffee apples.

On the Little Market place there was always the boxing booth, and the usual pugilists with the bulldog features urging the toughest of the bystanders to face them for ten rounds, standing with bulging arms akimbo, and looking as if a battering ram wouldn't budge them.

Dad was standing there one evening, laughing his head off at their antics.

"Dad - take me in to see them," I begged him.

"Alright lass, cum' on then. No, put yer' money away I'll treat yer'." And so we followed the crowd into the stuffy, enclosed building which smelled of sweat and sawdust.

Well - when the first two contenders started bashing each other about, the blood started to flow and the yobos in the crowd to shout and swear, I felt sick, and mumbling something to Dad to stay, I bolted for the entrance and the fresh air. I felt terrible, and I never went there again, ever.

On the Sunday night there was always an Organ recital. One of the largest of the Fair organs, situated opposite the Town Hall, would play a selection of popular classical tunes, and hundreds of people would be gathered around to enjoy the music.

The birds and young bucks would be parading round the Market Place, trying to 'get off' with each other. But I was too young yet to entertain such thoughts. Besides, I enjoyed listening to the classical music and watching the hammers and the cymbals banging away to produce the tunes. It was a fascinating display. We never have nights like that now during the Fair, do we?

And then on the Monday evening most of the Fair would start up again for a Grand Finale. All, or most of the proceeds would be handed over to The British Legion. Nowadays it's all 'catch pennies'; most of the prizes on the dart and coconut stalls not worth carrying home. Even the coconuts now appear to be nailed on.

Dad used to love to ride on the chairoplanes. This was a roundabout with a double row of chairs hanging from chain. As the roundabout gathered speed and momentum the chains, with their occupants, would be swung out over the heads of the spectators. I never went on that contraption – I was much too scared.

But I did go on the big wheel with Dad. I think it was the nearest I ever got to heaven. Oh – and the cake-walk. Now there was a ride on which you could get your money's worth. We'd keep dodging around behind people at the back of us, so we could stay on longer. Mind you – we had to be careful the attendant didn't see us or he'd soon be shouting.

"Git' along there – yer've had yer' penny's worth."

Mam never went on the roundabouts, she preferred to spend her money on 'summat she could see', brandy snap and gingerbread and she would always come back with a coconut.

The Peacock stalls were flourishing then. The stall would be laden with prizes and an overhead spinner with a brightly painted peacock at one end would spin around and a light travel up and down a screen full of place names. If the light stopped at your name, of which you had a counterfoil ticket, you'd won a prize, and could have the pick of the stall.

Ilkeston Fair

One day Mam came home with a lovely half-teaset in a box.

"They gave me a free ticket," she told us. "And I won this; i'nnt it nice, an' I never even spent a penny."

"But didn't you have another go Mam?" I asked.

"No fear," she declared emphatically, "They're not gettin' any money out 'a me." Yes, you can laugh, but near poverty had always made Mam careful about parting with her money.

Unbelievably, I still have two of the plates left, and that was more than fifty years ago.

Christmas was fast approaching and Aunt Ethel, who lived at Nottingham, had once more invited me to spend a few days with them. I was looking forward eagerly to seeing Cousin Gladys again, maybe going to the Panto and to a party, and maybe - maybe if it snowed in time - to go sledging on the Forest slopes. Oh I did love going to Aunty's; they had everything; green, plush covered chairs and sofa, a piano, lovely polished furniture and even a scullery indoors, with a tap, so that you didn't have to keep going out in the cold and wet every time you wanted a kettle of water.

And they had CARPET on their stairs. I began to get so excited I thought I would have diarrhoea. I did so want to go.

But a few days before Christmas I started to have the most agonising tummy pains, and one morning was horrified to see blood on my nightie. I searched to see where I had cut myself and, finding no scratch or wound, went into Mam's bedroom to tell her. Dad was downstairs at the time.

"Mam," I told her tearfully, "Look what's on me' nightie."

"Oh crikey! Ay' yo' started now," she grumbled. " 'Ere, better put this on yer'," and she gave me a baby's nappy and a couple of safety pins out of a drawer.

No explanation of what had happened, that this was a natural function, and would now be a regular monthly event. So back in my bedroom I struggled with the white square, folding it into a triangle as I'd seen Mam do before putting it under the baby's bottom. Yes - you can laugh. I told you I was naive, innocent.

"MAM," I called. "Where do I pin it."

"Fasten it to ya' chimmie," she answered in a stage whisper. "An' stop shouting. D'ya want everyone to know."

And that is how I came to adolescence, wanting to know about things, about life, but not daring to ask Mam to enlighten me further.

I knew Edie and Leshia would tell me next day at work. But this start of menstruation made me really ill – with shock mostly I expect, so Mam had to write to Aunt Ethel to say I'd not be over that Christmas. And so what a sad Christmas that was for me.

By this time the Wheatleys, our neighbours next door who'd had the chip shop, had left and a widow, Mrs. Wathey, opened the shop selling sweets and groceries. But soon she married a traveller, a Mr. Chadwick, and a year later a son Eric was born.

Mr. Chadwick used to run a market stall in several different towns. One day he asked Mam if I'd like to earn a bit of extra money, 4 pence an hour. I had to fill bags with tea from a crate, seal and label them. Another girl, Florrie Madeley, used to help, and Mam said I could have all the money I earned from this. So I was able to start saving.

But one day whilst I was at the factory Mr. Chadwick asked Mam if he could borrow my box of water-colour paints. He wanted to paint some price signs for his stall. Well, you should have seen those paints when he had finished with them, hollows gouged out of the lovely colours, paints smeared all over the trays. I wept, I railled at Mam, and I'm afraid the tea merchant fell a great deal in my estimation after that. But I swallowed my pride and still continued to pack tea for him. I needed the extra cash.

Besides I liked working with Florrie. She was a tall dark haired, handsome girl whom I looked at with awe. They lived at the top of a 'jitty' across from us. Florrie's mother had an artificial leg, and we could always tell when she was coming down the 'jitty', we could hear her leg squeaking. We kids used to laugh about it, called her peg-leg.

One day our employer asked us to tear off some sixpenny labels from some tea packets, and stick eightpenny labels on. I told Mam about it, I thought it rather a queer thing to do.

You should have heard Mam's comments; I will leave you to guess. But I told you I was naive, just thinking the previous packer had made a mistake. Anyway, the tea packing job lasted for quite a while.

One day one of my old school friends asked me if I'd like to go to a Social with her. It was only sixpence. But how could I, I'd got no pretty dresses to wear? I told Edie and Leshia, and they quickly came to my rescue. One of their husbands worked at the Celanese Works at Spondon, and frequently brought home bundles of remnants.

"Yer' can have a couple of pieces for a bob," Edie told me.

So I chose two pieces of yellow, artificial silk stockinette. The girls said they'd cut it out for me, which they did on the winding room floor. Two circular pieces, one for the bodice slightly scooped at the neck, and the skirt part joining somewhere around my hips. They even sewed it up at work, with me keeping watch at the door for any surprise visits by the big boss or the foreman.

I bought a big red artificial rose from Woolworths for a few pence, and hey-ho, I had my first party-cum-dance dress. But I'm afraid I didn't much enjoy the social and the dancing, for I was developing a terrible shyness along with my adolescence, and it seemed that everybody was looking at me – alone. I was so aware of my gawkiness, and along with a slight shoulder deformity, I felt a freak. I would avidly read every article I could on improving woman's appearance. I used to do all the skipping and bust improvement methods advocated. I washed my face in rain water, but still my spots and pimples remained.

Half my pocket money I spent on carrots, and raisins and oranges to beautify my complexion. But as the spots grew, so my ego deflated and I felt like the proverbial ugly duckling.

"What you want me'gel is some more brimstone and treacle," our Mam would tell me.

I was now without a pal with Elsie having a boy friend, and I would moppsubout the house of an evening and at weekends, which did nothing at all to boost my morale.

"Get ya' drawing book out," Mam would say. "I've not seen ya' do any painting just lately." But I did better than that. I decided to go to an Evening Art Class at the Grammar School. The other girls at the class were mostly the daughters of better-off parents, and some were not too artistically gifted. They would play about with leather, and metal, and be talking and giggling most of the time.

It seemed I was the only one who seriously wanted to improve my drawing skill, but I was painfully conscious of the fact that I was only the daughter of a common coal miner.

I was given books on figure drawing to study, with pictures of nudes adorning every page. I felt terribly embarrassed, especially as some of the other students would peer over my shoulder to get an eyefull of the luscious ladies.

I'm afraid I didn't stay at that class long, I was much too shy. But at any rate I had acquired a little extra knowledge about Art, and I had mixed with the 'elite'. But I was still lonely.

One day Mam said to me,

"I've asked Mrs. L. across the road if their Lily's got a pal yet, but she's still on her own; so yer' can both go out together. Better than moochin' about on yer' own so much."

"Oh Mam, what did you go and do that for?" I felt like a child again. But Mam was adamant, and so I had a new friend. It was Lily who introduced me to smoking. We were going for a walk one evening along the canal, and she suggested we bought a packet of fags. Two pence they were, Woodbines, 'coffin nails' we used to call them. There were five cigarettes, so that would be two and a half each. Well – we waited until we reached the canal and there was no-one about, Lily in charge of the fags. Then she opened the packet and passed me one. Tentatively I put it in my mouth whilst she lit a match and placed it to my cigarette.

"Go on – suck," she told me. I did, and instantly choked as the acrid smoke went straight down to my lungs. "Not like that you nit, just puff at it."

Eventually I got through my first smoke, but I didn't enjoy it one little bit. I felt so guilty, and kept looking around me to see if we'd been seen.

"We'll save these others until another day," Lily said. "We'll have to split the last one in half." It wouldn't have bothered me if I'd never, ever seen another cigarette as long as I lived. But I wasn't going to tell her that, I didn't want her to think I was 'chicken'.

And that's how I was introduced to one of the vices of life.

Chapter Four

Now that I was at work I didn't have so much time to go 'up town', shopping for Mam. Whilst at school Dan and I would go up to the Maypole shop for Mam's regular order: 1lb Mayco margarine, 8 pence, 1lb cheese, large tin Tarantella tomatoes, 8 pence, 1lb bacon pieces, etc. Then we'd call at Lipton's or Mason's for $\frac{1}{2}$ stone plain white flour and some balm (yeast). And we had to walk there and back, more than a mile each way. I used to love to watch the Maypole man patting the marg into place with his flat pieces of wood, and see the drops of moisture oozing out, and the narrow ridges on the patters making patterns on the pale yellow marg.

One evening in the week we'd traipse almost to the bottom of town again, to Glovers, the butchers on Granby Street, for hot savoury ducks; they call them faggots now. We'd take two basins, and oh my - didn't they smell delicious? And many's the furtive lick we had under the newspaper; but we only dared lick at the gravy. I used to love my supper that night.

But at the factory we worked on Saturday mornings, so Mam had to 'up town' on her own. There were lots of shops around us though, so Mam gradually got to using those.

There was Cockerams the butchers at the bottom of Bright Street. Mam would buy a large piece of brisket from there, and a couple of marrow bones for making dripping, and pork scratchings for Dad's supper. That was the furthest shop away from our house, in our immediate area. On the corner of Ash Street was Starr's the Pawnbrokers, 'pop shop'. They also sold bed linen, towels, moleskins for the pit, union shirts and pit boots, and a material called JANE for patching pit trousers, and then there were ladies vests and bloomers, and winceyette skirts and nightgowns.

21

We never used the pawnshop now, the Coal Strike was long ago finished. But I'd never forgotten the humiliation of going there with Dad's best suit.

Next door to Starr's was Jordan's the greengrocers. Mrs. Jordan was a pale rather tired looking woman, whom I remember, was very freckled. Mam got on well with her, which was saying a lot, for Mam was not given to making friends easily; maybe it was because Mrs. Jordan let her have things 'on tick'.

Then there was Hollis's, the pork butcher; typical fresh, pink skin, red cheeks, blue and white apron and straw boater. Mam used to get all her home rendered lard from him, and any bacon that was going cheap. I liked his scratchings better than Cockerams. They were square, delicious, rendered down portions of fat pork, a meal in themselves.

Next door was a barbers shop, a Mr. Blatherwick, one of Dad's drinking pals. Then came a pub, The Ancient Druids Inn, and a little further along a wet fish shop run by a Mr. Harold Henshaw, who kept a chip shop on the other side of the road. Mam always called him John Harold, as did everybody else. Then there were the Co-op shops, the butchers and the double-fronted grocery department. But we never traded there.

"Must think folks's rollin' in money," Mam would say. "Tha' gives thee divi but by God, tha' has to' pay it in fo'st."

A little further along, almost opposite to us was a Chemist, which we didn't use much apart from buying five-haporths, for the kids coughs in Winter, and Andrews Salts and Beechams Pills for Mam. She was, as I said before, a great one for cleanliness. Every weekend during the Autumn and Winter months when Dad was selling greens from the allotment, I would have to go across to the chemist's wife to ask what she wanted. It would invariably be 'nobby greens', brussels sprouts. Twopence-halfpenny a pound was what Dad charged. He would pick out the best and wash them under the tap, before I took them across. The woman always weighed them, and always grumbled that Dad watered them to make them weigh heavier. I hated going there.

Next door was another butchers shop, then came a wide opening with a row of houses running up an alley way. Next to that was a large 'white' double fronted house, with a wooden hut at the side where Johnny Wheatley, the cobbler, plied his trade. He lived at the white house. He was short, very stocky with stubbly, iron grey hair, and a mouth perpetually full of nails. I used to marvel as he transferred them in rapid succession to the sole he was hammering on. He had several sons, one was dark and as handsome as a film star, or so I thought at that time, as were his sisters with brown eyes and dark brown, curly hair. How I used to envy them, for mine was straight as 'pump water'.

Next to the cobbler's was Buick Sissons, the corn shop; but I've already told you about him in a previous chapter.

Next to Buick's was Dad's local, the Trumpet Inn. I used to pop into the outdoor sales for Mam's half pint of Shippo's: threepence or fourpence it was at that time. But I used to feel so embarrassed at going in there, as though it was a house of ill-repute. Maybe it was because a few rather loud-mouthed women used to be sitting in the passage. They seemed to be laughing and whispering about me. I was getting to be so shy and self-conscious.

Further along from the pub was another groceries shop – Jeffries, who were always noted for clean, quality groceries, especially on the bacon and ham side of the double fronted shop. They also had a barber's shop a couple of doors away, which the husband ran.

A few houses standing from the road and then another pub, The Jolly Colliers. They were a dry lot at Cotmanhay. This pub just formed the end of our shopping boundary.

Across the road from the pub was Mr. Fisher's, the draper, who was also a local preacher, and a collector for The National Deposit Friendly Society. This money was payed monthly at Wesley Street Schoolrooms, and provided money during times of sickness for there was no sick pay at that time, and doctors had to be paid for visits. No wonder so many people used to doctor themselves.

Mr. Fisher was a thin, grey-haired man who looked at you over the top of his specs. He was an upright, Christian man and greatly respected by everybody.

There were quite a number of houses then, fronting Cotmanhay Road before the next shop, which was a confectioners, Pembleton's. He was a pleasant little man, sprightly as a bird with a twinkle in his dark eyes, and with crisp, dark curly hair. His wife looked like a character out of Dickens, with her placid look, and an eternal mob cap on her head. I don't think I ever saw her without that cap. Come to think of it, I never, ever saw her outside the shop.

We often spent our halfpennies and pennies there; but we only ever got *just* the correct weight. I decided then that if ever I had a sweet shop I'd pop in a few extra sweets in each bag.

The Pembletons had two sons, and the eldest, I believe it was, took to music and formed his own dance band, and very well known he became in and around the Ilkeston area.

Another house and then a large shop front. This was occupied by Mr. Walters, joiner and undertaker. His premises were on the corner of Nelson Street, where his large workshop was situated. They were comparative newcomers. Before them there'd been a Mr. and Mrs. Williams who'd run a hardware shop. He'd gone around with a van, loaded and rattling with all sorts of chattels familiar with hardware, whilst his wife ran the shop.

But by the time I'd left school the joiner had moved in. I remember Mam telling Dad one day that the night before, quite late, Mr. Walters had come back from some party or other and run into the back of the 'night soiler's' cart, and got somewhat plastered with the evil smelling stuff. Mam thought this was hilarious, but I think she'd embroidered the tale a little with each repetition.

Sadly this man later took his own life. A man near by had also started a joinery business, and had undercut the true craftsman. I remember the morning well, when they'd found the poor chap hanging in his own workshop. He'd been such a nice fellow, and I felt extremely sad. This was my first experience of such a tragic happening, and I've never forgotten it, nor my anger for the usurper who caused it.

Across the street and next to our house was the Market tradesman, Mr. Chadwick. This wife ran the shop whilst he was out trading with his van.

Wheatleys, the chip shop people had been there before them. They were jolly, kindly people with four daughters. We were sorry to see them go, but glad to see the end of the pig swill in tubs at the bottom of our yard. Phew – the stench.

A few more houses then another shop – Annables, the cycle shop. We never had a bike so we never had any dealings with them, but they were nice, friendly folk.

A few more houses then John Harold's, the chip shop, who also sold fruit and vegetables. Mam would say:

"Some folk'us allus on the scrounge. Why can't they be content just selling chips, doin' Jordan's out o'business?"

"But Mam, people do as they like don't they? Anyway, I like Mrs. Henshaw, she allus picks me nice oranges out." At times Mrs. Henshaw had given me slightly speckled fruit, free – after I'd told her I'd bought it with my own pocket money, to make my skin nice.

"Yer've allus got to be opposite, haven't you?" Mam would answer. It was true, but I was a stickler for fair play, beginning to be really conscientious; a trait which has often been my undoing.

Next to the chip shop was another house, a covered-in entry and then Mr. Jones, the butcher. Just goes to show how much cheaper meat was in those days, doesn't it? All those butchers shops in a small area.

Mr. Jones was a thin, neat, bespectacled man, who was also a keen gardener. He had an allotment or garden some distance away, and was noted for his lovely roses. Many's the time I've seen him pushing his wooden barrow along, with a container covered with sacking perched precariously on it. I used to wonder what was underneath the covering, until Dad enlightened me one day.

Cotmanhay Road

"Why it's muck, fer' his roses," and seeing my look of inquiry, "Ya' know – the lavatory pan, out o'th closet."

I was astounded. I had never, ever, seen under our own wooden seat, never explored the dark cavity below. It sounds incredulous I know, but it is true.

When Mr. Jones retired his shop was taken over by a Mr. Dean, who sold wireless, gramophones, and recharged the batteries our radios ran on in those days.

That just about summed up all the shops in our immediate area, a distance of about a quarter of a mile.

Mam tried to run up a slate, "tick", at several shops, but some had a clear notice on the counter: *Please do not ask for credit as a refusal often offends.*

Mam would always send me to do the preliminary reconnoitring. I would object most firmly, but would have to go in the end.

There was a firm in Ilkeston who issued trading tickets. You bought, on credit, a ticket for two, three or more pounds, and traded your "ticket" for goods, usually at one of the shops "uptown". Mam bought all her bedding and towels, and our shoes and clothes this way. You had to pay so much back a week when the collector called, *and* a bit extra for the loan.

But Mam was never without a "ticket", and did most of her shopping at Rowell's and Wooliscrofts on Bath Street.

Nowadays they call it Hire Purchase, but basically the system is the same.

Once a year Mam would buy a piece of oilcloth, or American cloth to use it's correct name, for our kitchen table. This would be bought with the trading ticket, usually with the final bob or two at the end of her twice a year shopping spree. The table had a plain wooden top, and, over the years had become a bit uneven, the boards with which it was made producing ridges. With the washing and wiping which went on all day, by the end of a year the shiny oilcloth would be getting "tatty", and beginning to shred in several places.

When the new, patterned cloth was nailed in place, I would

look at it with as much pride as did our Mam. I don't think that today's formica tops could ever produce the same kind of enthusiasm.

Chapter Five

When Summer came around again Ede and Leshia announced that they were both getting married, and on the same day. Leshia's was to be quiet, family affair, but Ede had a long list of guests she had invited and I was to be one of them.

"I'll have to give her a present Mam," I said. "But I can't buy anything out o' my pocket money."

"Well – I've got now't to spare," Mam answered, then, brightening, "I know, give her one o' these dishes," and she proceeded to sort through the few items of glassware she had somehow acquired over the years.

"But Mam, they're not clean," I protested, pointing to the dust and stains which had collected in the cracks.

But Mam, ever resourceful took the best dish and scrubbed it thoroughly in warm soapy water until it shone.

"There ya', she'll never know but what it's new." But I felt awfully guilty when I presented my gift. Ede didn't seem to notice, thanked me warmly, and it didn't look too bad anyway among the other presents.

This was the first wedding reception I had ever been to, and I felt so embarrassed at some of the jokes being bandied about.

Now at that time, 1928, as soon as women got married they left work. It was the accepted thing that their husbands would now do the providing. The wife would cook and clean and start a family, her status now being a housewife and no longer a factory girl or shop or office girl.

So, my two dear friends had left, and two new juniors started. But I couldn't get on too well with one of the girls; she was related to the boss, and inclined to show her superiority. This I couldn't stand, so I searched around for another job.

After a few weeks I found one at Wolsey's at Kimberley. I'd still be silkwinding, but would now be on 'my own time', piece work as it was known.

Gosh – you should have seen those women work – talk about greased lightning. They would be 'niggling' away, casting hurried glances around at the others to see that they weren't getting ahead of them. With all the rush I felt a bit sick at first, but soon, I too was almost up to their speed. And when we were asked to work overtime, up to seven o'clock in the evening, I jumped at the chance for then my wage leaped up to £3 per week.

Now at that time £3 was a fabulous wage, just under £2 being the normal for a well paid job.

I felt so proud each Friday when I handed my wage packet over to Mam, for she was now able to save each week, and to buy things for the house, new wallpaper, a new window blind, and she could even afford a new felt hat and a coat for herself.

There were lots of people in our town who worked at Wolsey's, and we would catch an early morning train at the Great Northern station on Heanor Road. The fare was only a few pence return, and in ten or fifteen minutes we would arrive at Kimberley, pausing just long enough to pick up further passengers at the tiny Awsworth station.

A few minutes walk along the narrow main street and we would be at the imposing looking red brick factory. It was a clean, well run factory with a canteen for the dinner girls, as we were known. But most of us took our own sandwiches and flasks of tea. When we worked overtime it would be past seven thirty when we arrived home.

Talk about all bed and work. But wasn't I now doing what I had dreamed of doing for all these years, easing Mam's lot a little, enabling her to save a bit each week, something she'd never, ever been able to do before?

I still went over to Aunt Ethel's at Nottingham every month or six weeks. There was now a better bus service, but of course with mostly working on Saturday mornings I would have to travel during the afternoons. Cousin Gladys and I still went to the silent pictures at the Albert Hall; still cost us sixpence a night; and the elegant, swallow-tailed pianist still played the grand piano.

How I loved the classical music as his hands moved lovingly over the keys, a memory I have cherished over the years.

Wollaton Hall – entrance gates

On Sunday mornings Gladys and I would walk from Radford to Wollaton, and all the way around the extensive park, and often emerge from the entrance at Lenton.

Or we would explore, on Sunday mornings, the narrow, mean streets where now the Broadmarsh Centre is. One narrow alley, Narrow Marsh, used to house the sleazy book shops, the windows full of French novels, and square packets of something with just one name on the front. But at that time we didn't know what was in these mysterious looking packages. Gladys and I would speculate, evaluate, and I would repeat things the factory girls had told me. We would see gaudily dressed girls lounging about in doorways, all wearing more aids to their beauty than Nature had ever intended. They would stare at us insolently, and we somehow knew they were evil, but did not know why – not then.

Old Broadmarsh, Nottingham

Christmas that year I again spent at Aunt Ethel's. No tummy aches to stop me this time; and again we went to the Pantomime at the Theatre Royal. Gladys had booked the seats, and kept it secret until we were standing outside the place.

"This is your Christmas present," she told me as she led the way inside. What a show that was, the lights, the costumes, the dancing; and we viewed it all from the upper circle, and I tried not to look around too much, tried to act as though this was an every day occurrence. How I enjoyed these Christmasses at Nottingham, and Aunt Ethel's house was like Utopia to me.

Theatre Royal, Nottingham

A few months later our Dan was fourteen, and ready for work. There was no question about 'What would you like to do?' The Rutland Foundry was wanting boys, so that's where Dan went. He was thin and pale, it seemed cruel that he had to go out to work so soon. When I saw him one day after tea his left hand was bandaged.

"What you done Dan?" I asked him.

"I hit mi' thumb," and he took the bandage off, and I shuddered and retched. His thumb was a horrible mess, and he looked paler than ever when he managed to wash all the muck off his face.

But he was back at work the next day. I never really knew if he liked the foundry - he never spoke much about it. But he stuck it for years and years until he eventually went to the Erewash Foundry at Stanton. If he had dreams about doing anything else he never said a word about it - he just accepted things, same as I had to do.

It was May, and Sunday School Anniversary time again. I was now too big to go on the platform, for which I was profoundly thankful. Anyway, by now I had changed to Cotmanhay Church.

Mam would get all the vegetables for Sunday dinner ready early on THE day, so that she could sit behind the lace curtains and watch the parade. And what a parade. Ladies would turn out who wouldn't think of going to chapel at other times of the year.

They'd have their new coats on, and flower bedecked and beribboned hats, with dresses and gloves to match. Mam would stretch her neck to see the first of them come into view, then she'd move across to the other side of the window, to follow their progress.

"Else - come 'ere; there's Mrs. S. and her gel," she'd call. "I don't know where they get all their money from, dolled up'td nines."

Talk about a mannequin parade - and there was still the

return from chapel to be watched. Mam never missed a thing, and her comments were most caustic.

"Er stands need ta' go ta' chapel. Sunday Saints and weekday devils, that's what some on 'em are." Mam was what we used to term 'straight John Bull', no subterfuge at all.

I well remember a woman who lived a little way from us and across the road. She had one son and three daughters. Now the girls were always dressed nicely, though not too much to look at otherwise. This woman was forever extolling the virtues of her girls, and would say to Mam.

"There's not many gels look as smart as our'n when they're dressed up." Mam would seeth.

"Yer want to leave that fer other folks do you," she told the woman. "Praisin' 'em like that. Besides - 'andsome is as 'andsome does."

It wasn't often that Dad would pass any comments about anybody. He was so gentle - when he was sober that is, which was mostly during the week. He could see a bit of good in everybody. But one of his pet phrases was, "It's not a man's jacket 'as matters, it's what's underneath it." And how true that was - has always been. How wise he was.

One day when I got back to the factory after dinner, Edie said to me,

"I've just seen your Mam at a funeral,"

"Where? I asked, surprised. She'd said nothing to me about a funeral.

Why - that young woman's 'as got rid of 'er baby. You should have seen all the women standing around." It appears a woman had brought on her own mis-carriage by using a darning needle and things had gone wrong.

"Know what ya' Mam said to me?" Edie went on. "She said 'ah' stand need to go an' see a bugger like that, don't I?"

"What did she go for then?" I asked.

I used to hate anything like that, morbidness, any sort of nosiness, so this was a side of Mam I didn't like.

One day when I was walking down Bath Street with her, she turned round to stare at a gaudily dressed woman she knew, who had just passed.

"Well - er looks a right mess," Mam said. "Jus' look at 'er from t' back." But I wouldn't turn round - what bad manners. Mam was mad at me.

"What's a matter wi' yo'. Think yersen' somebody don't ya?"

But she was a good Mam really. Always liked me to have a new coat each Summer for best. Last year's coat I would wear for 'shifting in'; second best, to be worn in the week.

I well remember a royal blue coat I had, with a bit of black fur on the collar. At that time Rudolph Valentino hats were fashionable, those big brimmed, round hats worn by the famous Movie star. I had a black one, but when it was windy I had difficulty in keeping it on, and the big round brim would catch on the fur collar, making me push my head forward. I was glad when that fashion went out.

By this time black stockings were fast disappearing and lisle stockings had taken their place, and also shiny, artificial silk stockings. But they weren't as attractive as today's nylons.

Shoes too were getting more colourful, with shiny, patent leather, and hard wearing snake skin. I'd got long, thin feet but Mam bought me the round-toed styles because they were cheaper.

But it took me ages to get a new pair 'broken in', resulting in extremely painful blisters on my heels, and malformed feet in later years. How I applaud today's wise young mums, who regularly have their children's feet measured, and buy well-fitting shoes.

Chapter Six

When I had been at Wolsey's factory about two years, and feeling secure and happy becuase of the extra overtime money I was giving Mam, an event happened which really shook me. A young woman who was twenty one, and working on a winding machine on an upper floor, *and* earning less money, complained to the foreman, a lay preacher and a very fair minded man, that it was not right that a seventeen year old should be earning so much more than her. After some deliberation I was put on her machine, and she on mine.

Well – try as I might, I could never earn more than thirty shillings a week. I was heartbroken. So too was Mam when I told her.

"This money's no bloody good," she told me. "Yer'd better look round fer' another job."

"Oh Mam ... do I have to?" I begged. But Mam was adamant and I started to search around. After a few weeks I was lucky. I found another winding job at George Beardsley's factory on Cotmanhay Road. The pay wasn't too good, but at least I didn't have train fares to pay for. It was a cosy sort of factory, not too many staff, and I soon made friends with several of the girls. The room I worked in got the nickname 'The old maid's shop', because of the number of confirmed spinsters who worked there.

The pay wasn't so good as at Wolsey's, and Mam was for ever 'moaning' at me to go the the Celanese works at Spondon.

"Pay's good there," she kept on saying. "Other girls wo'k there." I would shrivel up inside. I had a dread of going to a big works like Celanese – all those hundreds of people staring at me.

The vision would haunt me at night, and I vowed I'd never work there. Why I'd rather go 'out service'. I'd made friends with two girls, both named Ida, who seeing me on my own so much had asked me to go to the pictures with them, and for walks.

Saturday night pictures, first house was sixpence then. If you wanted to act grown-up and go second house you could pay a shilling and book. Depended how 'flush' you were with money. At first we queued for the early showing, but it got so noisy, and rowdy we decided we were too lady-like to stand among the louts, so we went second house.

Sunday evening was when the 'monkey parade' really got under way. From seven o'clock onwards there'd be a regular parade of lads and lasses, up and down Bath Street, the main street. The girls would be in their Sunday best, and the boys with neat suits, ties, and short back and sides hair styles. No parading round in tight trousers in those days, and never a sight of a pair of jeans on a boy.

There'd be plently of wolf whistles and cat-calls as the boys tried to 'get off' with the girls, and giggles as the girls passed them. Talk about 'ladding' time.

The two Ida's and I didn't go in for such behaviour though, and would walk much farther than the top of the town. Much farther. Away down Stanton Road and along Ladywood Road which wound through lush green fields and past several farms. There was a farm with white-washed buildings on either side of a lane, across from Kirk Hallam Church. That lane is now called Welbeck Avenue. A little higher up from the church was another old, broken down farm; Vine Farm, which now accommodates a row of fine houses.

There was scarcely any traffic then; just the occasional lone car or motor bike, and of course, push bikes.

When the Winter months set in we would pass vague shadows of other girls and boys who enjoyed a longer walk, and would get the odd 'how do?' until we reached the Umbrella Tree.

This was a ragged sort of Yew tree shaped, I thought, more like a Cedar of Lebanon, with flat, plate shaped branches; just like an opened umbrella - hence our name for it. It was a well-known land mark which, unfortunately, disappeared when the Cat and Fiddle pub was built, and the Wimpey houses beyond it.

Illustrations by
Eli Chamberlain; Maplebeck, Notts

When we reached the Umbrella Tree we'd turn round and walk back towards the town.

So - every Sunday evening, dark Winter evenings especially, we'd walk to the Umbrella Tree and back. I well remember a fashion which was popular at this time; men's fashion that is, during the Summer months. Oxford bags: wide, floppy trousers, mostly light coloured. With them the young men would wear tight fitting, dark jackets, and round straw hats – cadies, we called them, and Oh my! didn't they look dandies.

The well-dressed young bucks would strut along, their trouser bottoms flapping around their ankles like sailor bell bottoms.

I never, ever remember a youth or young man going out of a weekend looking scruffy, with patched up trousers. Their hair looked neat too, short back and sides; and they all wore ties.

During our long walks I don't recall that we ever 'got off', 'clicked', made a date with any of the fellows we passed. The Ida's were careful with whom they associated, and I was too shy to even look a boy full in the face, and don't know what I'd have done if one had approached me.

This then, was my life in the pre-1930s, long hours at work for a miserably small wage, pictures on Saturday nights, and occasionally in the week (if I'd any money to spare after buying my health foods, carrots and raisins) a walk to the Umbrella Tree on Sunday evenings, and other nights spent at home, either reading or drawing.

Mam had started going to the pub on Saturday evenings with Dad, and of course I was expected to mind the two younger ones, Harold and Marie. Harold was about eleven and Marie five. She was a sweet, chubby, pretty little thing, but Harold – oh my, he was a young Pixie, always doing something he shouldn't be doing, and I usually finished up giving him a slap.

Mam wasn't much used to beer and at first she would always have a 'thick head', a bilious bout next day.

"Oh God! here we go again," I would groan, "Not only Dad getting too much, now Mam's started it," and I would doubly vow that I'd never get under the influence. And I never did, not over-indulge at any rate.

Mondays would usually find Mam lying down, after she'd first taken a Sedlitze powder, a vinegar cloth across her forehead. What a waste of money, I thought; and me still hoping and praying for a sewing machine.

But one day Mam said to me,

"Mrs. Stirland's got a treadle machine to sell – says yer' can have it for half a crown.

At last my big chance. Mam gave me half towards the cost and I went down to the woman's house, a hundred yards or so below us. I had to wheel it back, and what a fool I felt, the blessed thing clattered like a traction engine, and kept getting stuck in the cracks.

Mam started rounding up all her mending, sheets to patch, and a winceyette nightie she wanted making. But – try as I might I couldn't get the blessed thing to sew.

"Yer've bi'n had," Mam told me. "Better take the bugger back."

I was furious, but as I hadn't handed the money over, did the only sensible thing. I trundled the protesting monster right back to it's former residence.

"But I've only just been using it," protested the former owner.

"Well, it won't work," I told her. But inwardly I was trembling.

I was a very timid creature at that time.

And so I still hadn't got my long dreamed of sewing machine.

Chapter Seven

The 1930s came in with the start of the years of the depression. But history was being made.

A woman named Amy Johnson flew solo from Britain to Australia, and how that stirred up the conscience of women.

A man name James L. Baird invented the first television, so that sight as well as sound was being recorded.

Women started to wear trousers. From the Continent came the fashion of beach pyjamas which soon became the holiday craze on our own beaches. Hiking became popular, and so a new fashion was born - shorts. But they were the just-above -the-knee variety.

We were still a long way from hot-pants. I used to follow these fashions avidly, but did not always adopt them.

The first helicopter was seen in London, but they were called autogiro planes then. Yes - history was being made at an alarming rate, It was about this time that greyhound racing became popular too.

Women's hair styles changed drastically; curls and waves becoming the rage with the introduction of permanent waving.

Mam gave me the money for me to have a perm. It cost about seven and sixpence at that time. This was her repayment for the hours of sewing I had done.

I had to go 'up town' to get it done, to the newly opened Phyllis Hallam's Salon on Station Road.

At last I'd got rid of my 'pump water' hair. Maybe now I'd get a boy friend. But when I tried to wash it at home, and set it myself it went all frizzy, like a gollywog, and I cried with frustration. So now my precious pocket money had to be stretched to a shampoo and set every two weeks.

The factory went on short time and Mam started to 'niggle' at me.

'There's other factories," she'd nag. "Short time d'unt pay'd bills."

"It'll not be for long Mam," I'd lie, but I felt a sinking in my tummy.

One of the two Idas solved the problem. She got a job 'out service', at one of the big houses in the Park at Nottingham. Her mother wasn't too pleased, but Ida had a mind of her own.

"At least it's something different," she confided in me. "I'm fed up with that ruddy factory." I admired her courage. I wished I'd had the nerve to do it.

On the days I signed on at the 'dole' Mam made sure I had plenty of jobs to keep me busy. We still hadn't any water in the house, washing was still done in the wash-house across the brick yard, and we still hadn't got a water closet.

Sometimes Mam would say, "There's a heap o' hoss muck in't street. Better tay'd bucket and get it in." I would do so, shamefacedly. I suppose I was getting to be a snob in my adolescence. But there was always a race to see who'd get to the steaming heap first; I think the neighbours must have been peeping from behind their curtains.

Up to starting work Dan and I would of out 'horse mucking' with a bucket and dustpan before we went to school in the morning. Cousin Gladys, from Nottingham thought it great fun, and would beg to be allowed to go with us on this most menial of tasks. This pastime was getting beneath my dignity now, but, not wanting to antagonise our Mam I would nip out, red-faced, when a horse had passed.

Short time working and the 'dole' were making me increasingly depressed, a situation made worse by Mam's constant niggling.

"Yer'll hae' to go t'ud Celanese," she'd tell me. Now the Celanese, as everybody round here knows, was at Spondon, near Derby; a huge works employing hundreds of people.

But I was determined I wasn't going to THAT place. I

couldn't face all those staring faces. Why I'd rather – I'd rather go out service. The more I thought about it the more determined I became to have a go.

But Mam was furious.

"Ya daft thing. Yer'll be at everybody's beck and call. Yo' get on that bus termorrow, an' get yerself off to Spondon. Out Service – ah've never heard now't so daft in mi' life."

But I didn't go to Spondon, I went to the Unemployment Exchange instead, to see if there were any domestic vacancies. I was sent to a house on Wharncliffe road, a Mrs. Jackson's. She was a rosy faced, pleasant little lady who quickly put me at my ease.

"I want a general help", she told me, "And I'll pay you five shillings a week; and your keep of course. You will eat in the kitchen after you've served our meals in the dining room."

She showed me over the house. A dining room, a lounge, large kitchen and enormous pantry (or so it appeared to me) a washouse, and a long, wide hallway. My bedroom was little more than a box room, but at least I'd have a room to myself at last.

Wharncliffe Road

But when I got home, oh dear, all hell was let loose. Mam ranted on at me, called me all the silly buggers she could lay her tongue to. But I was adamant. I'd always had this streak of obstinacy. I'd show her I could stand on my own two feet.

"Alright mi' lass, yo' go an' 'ave a bash," she told me.

"Only don't come running back 'ere, scratin'."

And so it was arranged that I should move into the house on Wharncliffe Road on the Sunday evening, because Monday was washday, and an early start planned.

It was March and bitterly cold, a few days off my eighteenth birthday. The cold, however, did not deter the good lady of the house from rolling the two large ponch tubs out of an outhouse, and on to the brick yard just under the kitchen window. Each tub was half-filled with hot water from the kitchen boiler, and the first whites placed in. Then, I had to start ponching, and after a few minutes, put these wet clothes through the mangle rollers, and then into the other tub of cleaner water for a further ponching.

The clothes were definitely clean after this double battering. But then came the rinsing, the blueing of the whites, the squeezing through the mangle rollers again and the pegging out on the clothes line.

After a while the good lady went indoors for a cuppa, said I seemed perfectly capable, and I was left on my own.

By now it had started to snow, a few flakes interspersed with slivers of rain. But I still ponched away, inwardly cursing myself for being such a fool to get myself into such a situation.

The tears of self-pity started rolling down my cheeks, and I could barely see what I was doing. Slowly the pile of soiled clothes dwindled, until by 11.30 I had at last finished, the tubs emptied and rolled away, and four lines full of clothes blowing in the fierce March wind.

"Come along in my dear," Mrs Jackson said, and placed a cup of hot coffee before me. "We'll have to start cooking dinner now." Dinner? I felt more like going to bed, I was so exhausted. But the good lady had such a gentle, kindly manner I just did what I was told.

And so I became initiated into the art of good house-keeping, good cooking and the correct way to do everything.

"I've prepared you a time-table to help you my dear," my employer said at the end of the first exhausting day. It read like this:

6.30 am: Rake out ashes, prepare and light fire. (This was in the huge, iron kitchen range.)

6.50:   Clean outside step. Clean front door step.

7.00:   Set table in dining room. Start to prepare breakfast.

And so it went on throughout the day, me nipping into the kitchen repeatedly to see what was next on the list. A couple of minutes lost on one job and I'd be rushing around frantically all day trying to catch up.

Those first few mornings I had to scrape away the snow and ice from the outside (street) step before I could scrub it. Talk about soul-destroying work. I was already wishing I'd never decided to go 'out service'. But I wouldn't give in; I was not going to give our Mam the satisfaction of saying "I told ya' so mi' gel."

Chapter Eight

By the end of the first week I was getting quite proficient at working to the book. Mrs. Jackson would compliment me on the porridge and the crispness of the bacon, and the neat, quiet way in which I served it.

Mr. Jackson would be off to the grocery store on Bath St. which he and his brothers owned, by half past eight. The little girl would be sent to school and the baby, a boy, put in a play pen. Mrs. Jackson's sister, a nurse, also lived with them, so I had plenty of cooking to do.

I was shown how to prepare and cook vegetables; the correct way to lay a dinner table; to prepare tea and supper trays. Tea consisted of brown and white bread and butter, and home-made jam. And on special occasions, when visitors came to tea, delicious sponges made by milady herself.

She'd shut the doors to the kitchen and absolutely forbid me to enter whilst she was whisking the sponge mixture - said draughts would make it go flat. So - I never did learn how she made the delicious confection.

I hated Fridays. That was the day when the whole of the kitchen range was 'flued out'. There were so many little round pieces of iron that had to be lifted off, and the long brush poked through. I had to sweep as far up the chimney as I could reach, after first removing the hooded 'bonnet'. I'd be sweating 'cobs' as we used to say, and with repeated wiping away the moisture with the back of my hand - well, I looked like the proverbial chimney sweep.

I needed a bath that night I can assure you, but oh! the delight of stepping into a real bath with hot and cold taps, and a plug to run the mucky water out; and I hoped that never again would have to resort to the tin bath in front of the kitchen fire. Bath night at the Jackson's was pure heaven.

One day a Mrs. Broughton was coming to tea. Now this good lady was the present Mayoress. Well – you should have seen all the preparations which went on – as though Royalty were coming. A few days previously Mrs. Jackson had taken my daintiest white afternoon apron and cap and tinted them with coffee – yes real coffee made from Jackson's famous coffee beans. The result was a delightful shade, and my employer was so pleased with the way I looked.

I had to practise answering the door, Mrs. Jackson being the pretend visitor.

"No – not like that dear, open the door wide, don't peep from behind it. We want to make Mrs. Broughton feel welcome."

The morning of the visit, Mrs. Jackson shut herself in the kitchen whilst I cleaned upstairs. She produced a couple of the lightest, fluffiest sponges I'd ever seen, sandwiched together with jam and cream. I secretly hoped they wouldn't eat them both, that they'd save a bit for this poor, little 'skivvy'.

Then it was time for me to get dressed in my brown afternoon dress provided by milady, and don my coffee coloured cap and apron. It was like dressing up in my younger days, and I felt a great sense of excitement and had to keep running to the lav.

Mrs. Jackson inspected my hands and nails, then all at once the bell rang and I moved quickly along the hall, whispering the words of greeting under my breath. I flung the door open wide.

"Good afternoon Mrs. Broughton, will you please er – er," But it was only the postman with a special delivery letter. Mrs. Jackson was behind me and we both laughed at my mistake. Then the bell rang again and this time it was the visitor herself, resplendent in furs and a stunning blue coat and hat. I did everything just right, and was rewarded with a grateful look from my employer. I served the tea, and was then able to have my own 'cuppa' in the kitchen, and later, when the visitor had gone, to sample some of the lovely cream sponge.

Every Wednesday and Sunday afternoon was my free, half day, and I always went home. But first I had to prepare two trays, one for tea and one for supper, with sandwiches and bread and butter, with the appropriate cups and saucers etc. These trays were covered with a cloth and left on the huge stone slab in the pantry. Then, when I got back in the evening the pots were waiting to be washed.

Mam too, would leave jobs for me, the clothes line to fetch in, sometimes a couple of windows to clean.

"Elsie, will yer' finish sewing this shirt fer' me, and d'you think yer' could pin a patch on this sheet?"

Years later I read that 'persecution is the commonest cause of all neuroses' and I was certainly beginning to feel the start of it. It seemed as if Mam was determined to extract her full 'pound of flesh'.

I began to enjoy living among the gentry, as I thought of it then, and Mrs. Jackson was kindness itself, even if she was a bit of a slaveddriver, a perfectionist, and I never, in all the time that I was there, heard any of that household utter a swear word.

Now in my four years of adolescence I was becoming increasingly more anaemic, and began to feel exhausted by the end of each day. Mrs. Jackson was really concerned and bought me a bottle of iron tonic. I told Mam.

"That's what yer' get fer' wantin' to go skivvying," was all the sympathy I got from her, so I stuck it out for several more weeks. But I grew more tired, more apathetic, and Mrs. Jackson was really concerned.

"I think I'll have to pack in this job," I told her. "I'm not strong enough."

"Oh but I'm getting so used to you," the good lady said. "I wish you'd reconsider it. Look – I'll give you an extra shilling a week. Make it up to six shillings." An extra shilling! I wavered – then thought of all the jobs I'd had to ggt through every day.

Mam had been right. I was nothing but a servant, a drudge.

"I'd rather you got someone else," I told Mrs. Jackson. "I like it here, and you are so kind to me, but I'm really not strong enough."

And so I finished 'out service', and knew I'd have to start looking for a job again. Mam was almost gentle with me for the first few days at home, but couldn't resist the jibe,

"I told yer' there'd be now't out service didn't I? Let 'em all do their own bloddy skivvying."

Chapter Nine

Shortly after that I got a job at a lace factory, Masons on Albert Street. I had to wind cotton from cones onto bobbins. It was similar to silk winding, but much dirtier; the cotton fluff stuck to your hair, your eyelashes and got up your nose. I hated it and felt choked all the time, and the noise was terrific. But it WAS a job.

I knew I would have to stick it out or Mam would be on to me about Celanese again. Then I heard that Beardsley's were on full time, so sheepishly I went and got my old job back ·gain.

One thing I liked about factory life was the feeling of comradeship among the girls and women. Of course, there were the 'tittle-tattlers' and the scandal-mongers, but one soon learned how to deal with these, and to know who were one's true friends.

Inevitably one or two girls harped constantly on sex – were forever telling dirty jokes, and these I tried to avoid. At this time I had never been out with a boy, so did not want my romantic notions about love being sullied with too many of the basics about the way of a man with a woman.

And so the next few years passed by almost uneventfully. We were still hard up at home, still had our clothes and house-hold goods on 'club' tickets.

Then I was twenty one, and wondering if this was to be the start of a new and exciting era. I had a few nice birthday cards from my Aunties at Nottingham, and also a mysterious looking parcel from Aunt Ethel.

I opened it, then stared in disbelief and wonderment at the lovely pink silk slip and matching French knickers. I'd never

EVER had underclothes that had matched before. Always worn interlock vests and bloomers, and either a cotton or flannelette skirt, or slip as we call them nowadays.

I was so thrilled with this, my only birthday present, that I took it to the factory to show the girls. Just imagine anybody doing that now – the sniggers and the winks there'd be. But I told you I was naive, didn't I?

As you can imagine, I only wore that set on Sundays, and very special occasions. But this lovely present endeared my favourite Aunty still closer to me, and a great affinity drew us closer and closer over the years.

As I've said before, I was a sensitive creature, hating the coarse, vulgar things in life, and Aunt Ethel had a gentle, lady-like quality, often making me wish SHE had been my own Mother.

We always had this affinity, this great love for each other, and she reached the grand age of 94 before she died far away in Seaton, Devon, a little gem of a place near to where her daughter retired to, in Lyme Regis. But the highlight of my year was when I could save enough money to spend a few, brief days with her.

I was still suffering agonies through shyness, and Mam was forever going on at me to "get 'dolled' up an' goo' out like other gel's".

At this time I was becoming increasingly aware of a young man who had started at the factory as an errand boy, along with several others. He was broad shouldered, with a strong rugged face, light haired, and to me, at that time the epitome of all my dreams. I absolutely idolised him; for me, only he existed, and I fervently hoped he'd notice me and fall in love with me.

But I was so skinny, with hardly a bulge anywhere, and even took to padding my brassieres, a garment I could well have managed without.

But Henry Wilson, as I'll call him (though that was not his real name) apart from the occasional "How do?" seemed totally to ignore me.

An older married woman whom I'll call Mary, and who let me use her sewing machine, was forever trying to 'put a good word in' for me, a practice much adopted in those days. Today's young misses don't seem to need anybody else to do their pushing, do they? How sure they are, how very selective.

But Henry spent a lot of time at Mary's, for he had few friends, and was a bit of a loner, a shy young man; so it was inevitable that he would eventually want to be my young man, my hero.

What a romantic fool I was at that time, my head in the clouds, my heart given forever to a boy called Henry, and I would try to be in the same place as he on country walks, and on Bath Street, our main street, for I got know his habits.

I was not wise to the fact at that time that to catch a fella it's best to let them do the chasing. Such wisdom came later.

But when I saw him walking towards me my heart would leap, and the colour flood my face, and I'd feel a terrific excitement as I tried to walk nonchalantly past him. And he'd look shy and mumble "How do?", and I'd try to read into those two words a fervent longing for me; and when we accidently passed on our way to the factory lavatories I decided that Fate was definitely lending a hand, and I'd be flushed with happiness for the rest of that day.

This state of affairs was to last several years, but I often wonder how many really nice young men I must have totally ignored in my oblivious love-sick euphoria.

And so the year wore on, me in my dreamlike state and going about more and more on my own, in the hope that Henry would take pity on me, and ask me to be his girl.

Christmas was fast approaching, a season I looked forward to more and more, because I was now able to save a little each week, and would be able to buy Mam a better present.

It was usual for each of us to buy a present for the other members of the family, even if it was only a bag of liquorice allsorts, or a bar of chocolate for Mam, and bulls-eyes for Dad. We'd put all our gifts in a sack, and I'd be Santa, dressed in my

Bath Street

red flannel dressing gown, a recent acquisition bought with Mam's 'club ticket', and I'd pass one present at a time and the recipient would have to open it before I'd delve into the sack for another one.

There were six of us with Mam and Dad, so that was thirty-six little packages to be handed out. Of course, from the youngest, Marie, and Harold, theirs would be little, home-made gifts, for they were still at school.

But what an hilarious hour we had, oohing and ahing at the unexpected gifts.

But on this particular Christmas I was going to give Mam a real surprise. Now up to this time Mam had had a rocking chair, one without arms which was now, sadly, the worse for wear, for hadn't it rocked five babies to sleep over the years?

I'd secretly been gloating over a fireside chair, with padded back and seat, and broad, wooden arms. It was priced at £1.10 shillings. On the wall behind the chair was a mirror, an over-mantle as we used to call them. I told Dad about the chair and the mirror, and that I'd wanted to buy the chair for our Mam. He said he would buy the mirror, and gave me the money for it.

So back I went 'uptown' full of elation to order the goods before someone else had the same idea. The salesman at Greaves said he'd see that they were delivered on Christmas Eve. I could hardly contain myself for the next two weeks, and was sure Mam must have detected something.

Then the day before Christmas one of the staves broke on Mam's rocking chair, and she decided it was not safe to sit on.

"No use asking ya' Dad ta' mend it. He'd only mek' it wos'. Ah'sall hae' to save up fe'r a new un."

I was secretly rubbing my hands together in anticipation of the next day's events, and would love to have been at home when the goods were delivered; but we had to work through the afternoon of Christmas Eve.

Now at that time it was the accepted thing that factory girls would have a 'fuddle' at Christmas, and always on Christmas Eve.

A few weeks beforehand we'd start to put money into a 'kitty', and two of the older women would plan the eats and drinks. It seemed to be a major decision whether to have ham or tongue in the cobs, and this debatable matter was put to a vote. The trifles were bought from a local confectioners, already made in containers. There'd be mince pies, sausage rolls, a pear each, and a box of chocolates to pass around. And of course there'd be port and sherry.

There wouldn't be much work done that afternoon, I can assure you, the spirit of Christmas already in our blood, the sound of carols rising above the rattle and swirl of the winding machines, for we factory girls loved to sing.

At about 3.30, two hours before knocking off time, we'd raise our bobbins off the wheels, apart from a few empty ones to make a bit of a clatter, then we would sit in a corner of the room, out of sight of the door and start our 'fuddle'.

By the time 5.30 came round we'd be feeling very merry indeed. There were about a dozen of us in this particular winding room, mostly single women, 'the old maid's shop'. At about half an hour to finishing time, our foreman would saunter into the room, ostensibly to see that all was well but in reality to see if there was any drink doing. Sometimes our 'fuddle' collection had run to a small bottle of whisky, so we made sure we'd saved him a drink. And of course we had a sprig of mistletoe to catch any unwary male, mostly errand boys, who ventured into the room.

Some of the girls would meet at a pub later in the evening, but I'd never been one for 'pubbing', so I made my way home to help Mam with the baking, and the general preparation for Christmas Day.

But on this particular Christmas Eve, Mam's bonny face was lit up with scarcely contained happiness.

"Why di'nt ya' tell me about that chair?" she said. "A' made a right fol o' mi'sen when that chap brought it."

"Why Mam, what happened?" I asked.

"Well –" she paused for emphasis, "Ya' see the back was

folded down and it di'nt look like a chair. Ah' se'd tu'd man 'I ain't ordered no night commode'."

"Oh Mam," I burst out laughing – at the expression on Mam's face. "What did he say?"

"He said 'it's not a commode Missus', – I'nt it luvly' " and she went to it like a Queen to a throne. And that's what she looked like; a Queen on a throne.

I felt a huge lump form in my throat, but I also felt a great surge of happiness, for wasn't this what Christmas was all about – for giving.

Our Dad's present of the mirror lay open on the table, awaiting to be fixed over the mantle piece, and Mam kept picking it up to admire it.

That Christmas still stands out in my memory as one of the best I'd known. I did my usual Santa Claus act on Christmas Day, with the sack full of little packages beside me.

Mam sat proudly on her throne and Dad sat at the other end of the fireplace in his armchair, contentedly puffing away at his pipe; Dan and the two younger ones, Harold and Marie, eagerly awaiting their presents.

Then, when all the excitement had died down, the paper and string put in the dustbin, we had a carol sing-song, Dad's deep bass voice booming out above the rest. Dan was blowing through paper and a comb, and Harold was trying to get a tune out of his tin bazooka. Of course, having no piano or other musical instruments we had to make our own sound and what a cacophony it was.

Later on Dad went for his usual walk and I helped Mam prepare the stuffing for the pork. She always made her own stuffing and mincemeat and Christmas puddings as did most of the women at that time.

When the joint was sizzling and roasting away, and the potatoes and sprouts and large iron saucepan containing the 'plum pud' all simmering on the hob, Mam and I sat back and sipped a glass of sherry. Yes – we could now afford a bottle of port and sherry, now that Dan and I were both at work.

Dad didn't stay long at the pub that day, and was back in time for dinner, and when we'd stuffed ourselves full and the dirty dishes were cleared away Mam sat and read us Christmas stories from the Nottingham Guardian. It was a lovely Christmas Edition full of stories. It was the only time Mam bought the paper; her literary leanings being towards the Daily Herald, the Ilkeston Advertiser, and a few French novels she managed to borrow off somebody, and which she frequently hid under a cushion on the sofa.

Our Dan sat round the table and played Ludo, and Snakes and Ladders with the two youngsters, and I sat in a state of euphoria, drowsy with food and wine, and enfolded in a feeling of complete happiness.

What a wonderful sense of belonging, of being one of a family, of celebrating the birth of a special baby who was born some thousands of years ago. They were indeed happy Christmasses at that time.

Family and Aunt Mimmie, 1934

Chapter Ten

In the earlier part of the year Mam announced that she was going to try to save enough money to take her back to her birthplace, King's Lynn. It was here that she, and her sisters, Lizzie, Minnie and Ethel were born, and their only brother Bob. But their mother had died at an early age, after Ethel, the youngster was born, and Robert Tungate, their father soon found solace in a 'housekeeper'.

The eldest sister, Lizzie, a dark haired, brown beauty very gentle and lady-like in manner was, by this time married to Arthur Green, and when Mam decided to re-visit her birthplace, it was to stay with Aunt Lizzie and Uncle Arthur, who were now licensees of The Cheshire Cheese, one of the oldest pubs in King's Lynn. A supermarket now stands in it's place.

After Mam's mother had died and the housekeeper, whom they now looked on as a step-mother made it clear that they were an encumbrance, the three younger girls went to live with an Aunt Fanny and Uncle James, a brother of Robert's who also lived at King's Lynn.

These two dear people had not been blessed with children, so they were only too pleased to have the girls. Young Bob was by this time married to Charlotte, and they lived in a terraced house near the docks, at the north end of Lynn.

The girls stayed with Aunt Fanny and Uncle James for many years, until they all decided to seek work and a home in Nottingham.

But the three sisters were unanimous in their dislike of 'tho'ode gel', the stepmother who'd literally forced them to seek a home elsewhere.

Each week then, from the start of that year Mam would give

me a few shillings to save for her. She distrusted banks, and I could never make her see that they were not out to 'do her down', and that she would ultimately benefit from the interest they paid out.

Dad said he could look after himself, and Dan and Harold, for a week, so that I was free to go with her, and of course we'd take Marie, the youngest, with us.

Came the holiday and Mam had baked a number of loaves, which she put in the pancheon on the floor of the pantry, two big fruit cakes, several apple tarts on plates and a huge iron saucepan full of stew.

"Thi' not starve if thi' gets that lot on thi' chest," Mam announced.

And so we set off with a small suitcase, borrowed, filled with bare essentials, night clothes etc. We caught a train at the station at the bottom of Bath St. And changed trains at Nottingham. It was the longest train journey I'd ever been on, and I was so excited I thought I'd have the usual diarrohea. But everything went smoothly and in a few hours we saw the spire and turrets of St. Nicholas and St. Margaret's churches, beyond the broad sweep of the river Ouse. Fancy Mam wanting to leave a beautiful, historic place like this to live in Nottingham.

We walked from the station to The Cheshire Cheese, and Mam was pointing out of places of interest with more than a few tears in her eyes. Of course, we got a warm welcome from Aunt Lizzie, but I was surprised to see that her hair was white, and that she was carrying a large bucket of coal from a door at the back to the stairs which led to their living quarters above.

"Ya' shouldna' be doing that," Mam said. "Where's Arthur?"

"Playing dominoes with his mates," she nodded towards the tap-room. "You have to keep the customers happy," she said in a gentle voice.

I'd have been seething had I been in her place, and I'm afraid Uncle Arthur fell a great deal in my estimation after that.

Next day Mam took me around the old town, and I was enchanted with the place, with the old gateways, and the twin turreted St. Margarets Church, and the flood level marked on a pillar before the altar.

Flood Levels at St Margaret's Church, Kings Lynn (now moved to main entrance)

Then I met Uncle Bob, a short, thick-necked man with a red face and cheerful manner. Aunt Charlotte was thin, dark and didn't laugh much, and only gave me a peck for a kiss, and the meal she gave us was very frugal indeed, for I had an enormous appetite. Aunt Charlotte had two lodgers 'Horry' and Peter, who both worked at the docks at the North end of Lynn.

Peter was very young, even boyish, but 'Horry' an older bachelor was a big, friendly, tow-headed man. He told me he'd take me round his dock the next day - show me the ropes.

It was a truly wonderful experience to see the boats from Sweden and Norway unloading their cargoes of wood. Then there were the cockle boats to watch, and 'Horry' pointed out a canning factory on the other side of the river, and I could just make out the workd *Lincan* on the roof.

After that Mam took me to see Aunt Fanny and Uncle James. Aunt Fanny was round and comfortable, and gave me a big hug. I took to her straight away.

"Just fancy Nellie," she said to Mam, "You have a family growing up fast," and the tears came quickly to her eyes.

Uncle James was slender, stooped a little and had thick white hair, and a white goatee beard, and the gentlest manner. He made me think of a Saint.

Our Dan

He used to be a carpenter, he told me, and had once sent Mam a big, mahogany blanket chest for a wedding present. I have the chest to this day. And he'd even sent Mam a dulcimer, a musical instrument he'd made. But sadly we'd broken it in one of our rough games.

"I'll take you to see my garden tomorrow Elsie," he told me. Sure enough next morning I walked beside this venerable old man down the cobbled street and across a main road to the gardens, hidden behind thick, high hedges.

I have never seen such a tangle of vegetation, struggling for supremacy. There were blackberry brambles mixed up with the runner beans, and marigolds making splashes of bright colour among the potato plants, and peeping from amongst the muddle a wooden shed, leaning at a crazy angle.

But there was the song of birds everywhere, and the drowsy hum of bees, and a feeling of seclusion and utter peace, a sense of being in the presence of God.

Uncle James potted about whilst I lost myself amongst the tangle, and later he produced a flask of tea and home-made, carraway seed cake; and we sat on a rickety old seat in front of the shed, in the warm sunshine, and he pointed outt the various birds and butterflies, and I listened to him in wrapt adoration.

And when later I founda piece of cardboard in the shed, and wrote on it in large letters 'You are nearer to God in a garden than anywhere else on Earth' and propped it up inside the shed window, there were tears in the old man's eyes.

"You're a good lass Elsie, I wish we'd had a daughter like you," he paused. "Aunt Fanny and me were wondering if you'd like to stay and live with us. Ask your Mam, we'd love to have you."

I could scarcely take in his words.

"You mean – live here all the time?" I was quiet for a long time. "Oh I don't think Mam would let me. Besides –," I thought for a moment, my mind going in circles, "Well – you see Uncle James, I work at the factory, and my money helps

Mam a lot now. She's only just been able to start saving."
Uncle James patted my arm.

"I understand my girl. Of course she wouldn't want to lose
you, not now. Well - we'd better think about getting back
home." But that day a wonderful link of affection had been
cemented between us, which was to last for a long, long time.

For several years after that a large box would be delivered to
me containing various sorts of apples and pears, even blackber-
ries, and more often than not a bunch of limp flowers on top.
And there'd always be a letter pushed in with the fruit, 'To my
dear Elsie'.

"Oh bless him, the old dear," I'd murmur, as I opened up
the treasure box, scarcely seeing what was inside through the
blur of tears.

We corresponded for several years after that. Poor Aunt
Fanny died about two years later, and Uncle James plodded
along, looking after himself, the cottage and his rambling old
garden which was across the busy main road, opposite the
cemetery, which he visited every day, he told me in one of his
letters.

"I do miss her so." He took flowers from his garden for the
grave. "I cry so much when I've been there, sometimes I can't
see where I'm walking."

So it came as no surprise when Aunt Lizzie wrote to Mam
and said the old man had been knocked down by a motor bike,
and had died on the way to hospital.

He was laid to rest by his wife's side, and I felt very sad for a
long time after that. For this white haired old man was truly a
saint, and I was proud and happy that I had known him. And
so ended another chapter of my life.

Chapter Eleven

After this holiday with Mam at King's Lynn there followed a
period of intense heartache for me. As I've told you before I
was very shy, painfully so at times, which was increased by the
awareness of my extreme thinness, and a slightly deformed
right shoulder which, I thought, made me look a hunchback
from the side.

By this time the two Idas had decided that two's company
and three's a crowd so I was on my own again. Oh - we were
still friends, but never being one to push myself I accepted the
situation without demur. So - when I went my lonely walks,
and to the pictures on my own, I had no-one to talk to, to
confide in.

Inevitably my thoughts grew inwards, and I would try to
analyse my every action, and why I felt so unhappy.

I was still love sick for Henry, and still saw him on some of
my lonely walks, but apart from "Ey up" and "How do?" the
situation remained the same. How he must have laughed at me,
at my pitiful attempts to get to know him better.

At this deeply unhappy time my periods suddenly stopped,
for months on end. I was scared. Could I be pregnant? But how
could I be when a boy had never even kissed me?

This only added fuel to my introspection until I was scarcely
aware of anything that was going on around me, apart from the
fact that everybody was staring at me, or so I imagined, and
this made me withdraw more and more into myself until it
became an effort to open my mouth to speak to even my Mam
and Dad. I'd become an introvert, without even realising at
that time the meaning of the word, and when I wanted to go to

the pictures I'd walk through the back streets until I reached my destination, and would slip almost furtively into the foyer of the King's or Scala or Ritz.

I was very, very unhappy, and at one period wished I could go to sleep and never wake up again, and I knew how a person must have felt before contemplating suicied.

In these enlightened times I'd have been referred to a psychiatrist, but Mam didn't seem to notice what was happening to me, apart from the occasional caustic comment.

"What's up wi' you? Frightened to oppen yer' mouth. Ya' want to try laughin' a bit more – ya' face's long as a wet wik'." This only made me feel worse. Oh dear God! Would this torment never end? The days dragged by at work, I imagined that the factory girls were whispering about me, and I scarcely spoke a word. Inevitably the other girls started ignoring me. I was a nobody – a failure.

This spell lasted for months and months; almost a whole year out of my life I realised later. Maybe this is why I now crowd as much as I can into each day, to help make up for the time I lost.

I used to pray to God each night for deliverance, for some miracle to happen that would make me be like other girls, carefree, uninhibited and enjoying life to the full.

And then the miracle happened.

The factory bosses at Beardsley's, where I worked, bought a piece of land at the back of Manner's colliery. It was quite a few acres, enough for a cricket pitch and several tennis courts. They rolled a section of grassed area and made two courts, and had another piece red gravelled for a hard court, and invested further in high wire netting. There was already a tattered looking pavilion which the men soon licked into shape.

All these facts scarcely registered in my numb, tortured brain. I couldn't have cared less at that time what events took place. Then Frank Bostock, one of the warp knitters, volunteered to teach any who were interested, how to play the game of tennis. The men also got a cricket team together, bought their whites and cricket gear and started to play, challenging other teams as they grew more profficient.

I was twenty two at the time, and it was late Spring, and I was feeling very sorry for myself, wishing that I could be more like other girls.

"Are you going to learn to play?" one of the winders asked me.

"I don't known" I was evasive. "What about rackets, and tennis balls?"

"You might get one second-hand. I'm going to buy a new one." I thought for a bit. Well – I might as well join them, what had I to lose?

I saw an ad. in the Advertiser, bought a racket second-hand, two brand new balls, and I already had white plimsolls which I wore when I went with Aunt Ethel to Ingoldmells.

At that time girls wore ankle length cotton dresses, or long pleated skirts with blouses; never a pair of shorts to be seen.

So – one Saturday afternoon – I set off, feeling very self-conscious, with my plimsolls tied to my racket handle, blushing furiously if anybody looked at me, and met a couple of other girls at the bottom of Charlotte Street. We walked up the hill, and then down by the side of the Ilkeston hospital and past Savage's farm to the sports ground below.

Frank Bostock and his young lady, Dorothy, were waiting for us. She could already play tennis. A few more girls and a couple of young men turned up, and I was surprised to see that Henry was one of them. I was painfully aware of his presence.

Frank showed us how to serve, how to volley, and when we got the hang of it, how to start counting. But I thought then and still do, what an idiotic way to count – all those loves, advantages and deuces. Why not a simple counting of points? The fresh air and exercise were wonderful, but the racket seemed to weigh a ton, and next day my right arm felt as if it would drop off.

There was a lot of squealing among the girls and a few swear words from the boys, but the afternoon passed so quickly, and I was so intent on getting my shots right I forgot to be shy.

"We'll have to finish now," Frank said. "Can you all come on Monday night?"

I felt full of fresh air, and absolutely ravenous with all the exercise, and better than I'd felt for months, and the fact that Henry Wilson had joined the players made me determined that here was something I was going to shine at.

"How did ya' go on?" Mam wanted to know.

"Alright Mam," I told her.

"Ya' look better already. I reckon it'll do ya' good."

Aged 25

After that we played most nights in the week, and every Saturday afternoon when it was fine. One night when I got back home, ravenous as usual, Mam said.

"Why don't ya' fetch ya'sen half a pint o'ale from Trumpet?" Beer was eightpence a pint then. Could I afford the fourpence for a half a pint, I wondered? Up till then I'd only tasted beer in small measures, a wine glass full pinched out of Mam's frequent half pints. It was a common practice at that time, especially among the colliers' wives to take a jug, or half pint mug to the outdoor sales at the pub.

Trumpet Inn

So - I fetched my half pint - it was Shipstone's mild, and when I got back in the house Mam had cut a plate full of thick slices of her home made bread, some hunks of strong cheese and rounds of Spanish onion. That meal tasted super to me, for I was 'famished', and the strong beer tempered the bite of the onion.

And so, each evening, after an energetic game of tennis I'd enjoy my supper of bread, cheese and onion and half pint of 'Shippos'. As my general health got better, so my mental health improved, especially now that we frequently formed a four-some with the boys, Henry Wilson included.

But I never realised until later years how near I'd been to having a complete nervous breakdown.

And so the Summer wore on, more of the factory workers joining in the tennis, and the men's cricket team; but always they joined us for tennis in the evenings.

Still Henry didn't ask me for a date, but we played some marvellous doubles, he invariably being my partner. Oh what bliss that was. I was in a Seventh Heaven of happiness.

Inevitably the Summer came to an end, and with the darker evenings we had to abandon our games for that year. But one of the girls said,

"Why don't we all keep together - go dancing, or summat'. It's only sixpence at St. Mary's dancing classes."

St. Mary's was the parish church, high on the hill by the Market Place, and it had a large, old school building near by, which catered for weddings, dances, scouts etc.

When I told Mam about the dancing idea she was all for it.

"Ah' keep tellin' ya' to goo' out an' enjoy yoursen', don't happen ya'll get a lad now."

Happen I would. So now we tennis girls arranged to meet on the Market Place the following Saturday, and go to St. Mary's. None of us had danced before, not proper dancing anyway, only to socials, so we were all looking forward to this new experience, wondering if it would lead to romance. I fervently hoped so.

A real "Bobby Dazzler"

Chapter Twelve

That night I went 'uptown' on the trolley bus which only cost a few pence for the mile and a half or so from Cotmanhay, to the Market Place - I didn't want to tire myself out walking up that hill.

The heavy, clanking trams had stopped running in 1931, the iron rails pulled up, the road filled in and trolley buses had started to run. The trolley buses were still equipped with an overhead pole, which contacted the electric wires above, but having tyres, were considerably quieter than the old trams.

I never envisaged at that time that by the 1980s almost every household would own a car, some of them two and three, and that we'd literally take our lives in our hands every time we crossed a road, or that there'd be passes under busy roads to get people safely to the other side.

And look at the advancement there has been in air travel, jets, travelling faster than sound. A vast difference from the old wooden, two winged structures. But I am digressing from my story.

It cost sixpence to go into St. Mary's schoolroom to dance. That would be from 7 o'clock to 10.30 p.m. with a half hour interval for refreshments. Sandwiches, potted meat usually, or egg and cress cost two pence, and trifle three pence a portion. There was a lady playing the piano for dancing. She was a Miss Cook, a local music teacher, and could play with a strict tempo rhythm. There was no dancing teacher, just an M.C. and he would select one of the better lady dancers to get the dance going, and lads would select lasses with a polite,

"Would you care to have this dance?" or a not so polite "How about it?"

I'm afraid I didn't get many partners at first – well, I was all feet, size seven into the bargain. So I invariably danced with one of the girls, but when it came to a Paul Jones I did sometimes get a male partner, but mostly only if we were the last two facing each other. Some of the boys looked very disappointed, and my ego took a nose dive. I was, as I have said before, very gawky and self-conscious.

The dance hall at St. Mary's was long and narrow. In a foxtrot you could manage a few, good long strides down the room, but it was so narrow you could just make a couple of steps across, consequently there was much bumping.

I liked the intervals best, with the sandwiches and especially the trifles. I've always loved to eat.

After that it was a regular thing to go to 'Mary's' as we called it, on Saturday nights, and when we grew more proficient we went to the Premier ballroom, and to the Miner's Welfare and the Town Hall. There was also dancing at the Ice Stadium, and at the Durham Ox, though I didn't frequent these last two.

Besides these dance halls there were four picture houses, all doing well, so there was plenty to entertain the lads and lasses and their parents too, with never a Bingo hall in sight. Silent pictures were now a thing of the past, as was the inevitable piano player providing the appropriate accompaniment.

We now had sound and rhythm, and gorgeous extravaganzas from Hollywood.

I still went to the pictures occasionally, and always on my own, but was now more 'taken up' with this dancing craze. I enjoyed the movement to music, the bodily expression of rhythm and this love of dancing has never left me.

Some of the more straight-laced of the community thought dancing abhorrent, an invention of the Devil, and that all girls who went dancing were 'tarts'. I was glad that Mam approved of it, or I'd never have discovered this joy of self-expression.

None of the tennis or cricket boys joined us at St. Mary's, but they did attend the Whist Drives organised by the factory staff, and held in the Mending Room on Friday evenings.

I didn't care much for Whist, but kept attending although all I ever won were several booby prizes. But you see Henry was there and another chance for me to say 'hello', and for him to pluck courage to ask me out. Mam knew how I felt about him.

"He'll ask you out afore long – you mark my words," she'd say, but still nothing happened.

I continued to go round to Mary's room, to use her sewing machine; she knew all about my 'crush' on Henry, and did all she could to bring us two together. He often came round for a bit of companionship whilst I was there, and although Mary threw a lot of hints about what a long way it was for me to walk home, he – just never took the hint. He told Mary one day.

"Oh Elsie's a nice enough girl but she's so – so thin." After that I started to eat more fattening foods, more puddings, and even took to arm swinging exercises to try to increase my bust. But still I remained as thin as a rake.

One day Mam said to me,

"D'you think Mary 'ud like to 'ave a bowl o' broth wi' us? Ask her; then she can come back wi' ya' on Wednesday dinner."

In the Winter months Mam always made broth on Wednesdays, with the bones and scraps of meat left over from the Sunday joint of brisket. Monday would be cold meat day, and Tuesday would be hash, with onions, potatoes and carrots.

Mam often made sudden kind gestures like this. I felt suddenly very warm towards her, because Mary had no young men friends, was well into her thirties and had an eye affliction, loss of eyelashes. But she had a heart of gold.

So – every Wednesday after that, during the cold weather she walked the half mile home with me. Mam got on like a house on fire with her, and Mary was forever extolling the virtues of Mam's broth.

One day, one of the factory girls whose name was Grace, a very popular girl with the boys, and who often joined us girls for dancing said to me,

"I've just had a couple of tickets given to me, for the Police Ball. Would you like to go?"

The Police Ball! One of the biggest events of the season, AND at the Town Hall. Would I? I most certainly would, and I felt a tremendous excitement at the thought of it. But - what would I wear?

At all the big dances floor length dresses were worn, but Mam came to the rescue, good old Mam.

"They've got some nice frocks up at Clarke's," she told me. Now Clarke's was one of the elite shops on Bath St, just above Chapel St, where a pork butcher now stands. So the following Saturday we went 'up town' to the dress shop, and I self-consciously tried on several long dresses. But they all seemed to be cut into a deep V at the back, a fashion very popular at that timem I'd never get one of those to stay on my shoulders.

There was a gorgeous flame coloured dress, floor length and with two ruffles round the top of the arms and bottom of the dress, and with a broad sash. I tried it on.

"But you can see me' vest Mam," I told her in a whisper, twisting myself to see the back. But it was a lovely dress, and looked good on me, for I had black hair then. The assistant came to the rescue.

"But Madam we can soon alter that," and she picked up the sash. "Look - we can take a piece off this and make the back higher."

Which is what they did. So at that Mam paid the money, one pound and ten shillings, which was the most she'd ever paid for a dress for me. How I loved that dress. It seemed to make me sparkle, to feel more self-confident.

Came the night of the Ball, and I'd had my hair Marcel waved and curled at Phyllis Hallam's, 'uptown'. I was so excited I had to keep running to the 'lav', and Mam was flapping around me like an anxious hen.

"Ya' want to put a bit more colour on yer' cheeks," she told me. How things had changed from my first carmined days. I got out my small bottle of 'Evening In Paris', a Christmas gift from Mam, and dabbed it discreetly at the back of my ears and on my wrists, as it told you in the women's magazines.

I felt very self-conscious as I walked along Cotmanhay Road my long dress showing beneath my knee length coat. I felt like a debutante going to her coming out ball.

Grace's home was on my way 'uptown' and I wondered what she'd be wearing. Her dress was black lace with net sleeves, and she had one red, artificial rose pinned into the deep V at the front. Her warm gold hair was fluffy and shining, and her cheeks glowed with good health. She looked radiant, and I felt a momentary sinking in my tummy. Who'd look at me with Grace by my side?

But I soon forgot my qualms in the joy of the music, played by a real orchestra, and in gazing at all the lovely dresses, the elegantly waved hair-dos, and the 'bobbies' and other men in their black dinner jackets, and spotless white shirts.

At that time the ballroom at the Town Hall looked huge, made even more so by the white lace, almost floor length curtains at the windows.

Grace was soon 'collared' for a dance, and I felt the first stirrings of panic. Then a voice behind me said,

"May I have this dance?"

He was tall, dark, and very friendly, could dance well and soon put me at my ease as we waltzed and foxtrotted, and I kept catching sight of myself in the long mirrors. I liked what I saw.

Grace never lacked a partner, and I was completely monopolised by the young man, who told me that he had chauffeured the Police car which came from the Long Eaton and Sandiacre district.

Of course, I did full justice to the trifle at the Interval, and by that time had decided that this was the best evening's dancing I'd ever had.

I never saw the young man again until the following year at the Police Ball, when he again asked me to dance, and partnered me for most of the evening. These dances went on until 2 o'clock in the morning, after which we had to walk back home. But we were never afraid of being molested at that time, and many's the time I have walked back home at midnight on my own. But then, I would walk down the middle of the road, avoiding the dark door ways. I was taking no chances.

And so the Winter wore on, me going to dances several times a week with one or other of the factory girls. And although I was occasionally asked to dance I was never escorted home by a boy, and never at that period, asked for a date, for I was still moonstruck over my first love.

Chapter Thirteen

Another year crept by, Spring seeing the end of our dancing, and the anticipation of our carefree, tennis days again.

Whitsuntide, and a crowd of us girls went to London – the first time I'd ever been to the capital. It was scorching hot – London seemed deserted, apart from the visitors, and we were glad to get into the coolness of St. Paul's Cathedral. Madame Tussaud's was spooky, and made me feel sick; but I loved the River Thames and St. James Park, and felt very patriotic as I gazed through the railings of Buckingham Palace.

What a lovely day that was.

That Summer the weather was glorious, and we again played tennis every Saturday and most evenings in the week. I felt wonderful, healthy in body and in mind, and seemed to get on well with all the others who played, the boys as well as the girls. But still Henry did not ask me to be his girl, although we played frequent games of tennis together.

My younger brother Harold, who was now sixteen decided to join the Army. He had tried several jobs since he'd left school, but did not seem to settle in any of them.

"Ah should'na goo' in th'Army if I was you," Dad told him. But Harold had made up his mind. So – off he went – to Catterick I believe it was.

Mam was really upset – even more so when she had a letter from him after only a few days.

"I can't stand this life Mam, it'll drive me mad. You'll have to pay to get me out. I think it's twenty pounds." At the end of the short letter he'd written, 'If you don't get me out I'm sure I'll end it all.'

"Oh dear God," Mam said. "What'll ah' do?" Twenty

pounds – it's a fortune." It was to her – then. She'd been giving me money to save for her, a few bob each week. As I said before, she distrusted banks, and I knew she'd just got £21 in the little tin cash box.

"Elsie, how much 'ave ah' got," she wanted to know. "Ah shall hae' ta' buy him out."

"Oh no Mam – not ALL your savings," I reproached her. "No – I'll not let you do it. He'll not do 'owt to himself – he darsn't".

"Gimme' that money," she demanded. So grudgingly I handed it over.

"I shan't save you any more money our Mam," I told her, and really meant it at that time.

And so about a week later a very sheepish looking Harold arrived home.

"You shouldn't have took any notice o' that letter I sent," he calmly told our Mam. Dear God! I thought she was going to have a fit.

That was the only episode to an otherwise happy Summer.

Two of the winders, close friends, said they'd like to have a holiday in Wales, at a holiday camp. Now holiday camps were a new innovation at that time, 1935, and this one at Abergele was the only one in that area.

One of the girls, Ivy Henshaw, asked me if I'd like to go with them.

"Bertha's taking her sister. D'you think your Mam would let you take your Marie," she asked me.

"I can ask her. I'd like to go anyway." Marie was eleven years old then, a slim, shy, pretty girl, very gentle in manner. Mam was all for it.

"Ya'll look after her well won't ya' Elsie?"

" 'Cause I will Mam."

And so off we went to Wales. All the small railway stations were open then AND showing a profit. The line at Abergele ran right alongside the beach, and we were able to marvel at the miles of golden sands.

What a week we had. The accommodation was in caravans and meals taken in a large hall. Ivy and Bertha Smith and Bertha's sister, and Marie and I would take long walks along the beach, singing at the tops of our voices, and shouting sly remarks to youths who were playing football on the sands. "How's your father?" was a saying much bandied about at that time. Now who was the comedian who made that saying famous?

One day we went to Llandudno and climbed the Great Orme, but Ivy and Bertha and the sister had had enough at the half-way mark, so Marie and I carried on to the top alone. What marvellous views we had from that vantage point, the pier on the one side and Conway Bay and the estuary of the River Conway on the other.

It was the first time I'd gone without Mam and Dad, and the lack of parental control made it all the more exciting. But, inevitably it was time to go home. All good times come to an end.

But back home there were the tennis courts waiting, more golden hours in the sun, more games with Henry, lots more happy weeks to enjoy.

What a happy, memorable year that was, and there was still the dancing to look forward to when the dark nights closed in.

Grace and I had formed a regular friendship by this time, so we started going to St. Mary's dances together.

There were a couple of young men who'd started to go too, and who showed a marked interest in us both. They wore neat, dark suits, spotless shirts and nice ties, and had shining, well combed hair.

Tom, the one with black crinkly hair and dark eyes, a typical lady-killer, showed a marked preference for Grace.

The other young chap, John, was also dark, with smooth hair, a rather broader face, and had a broken nose, the result of a childhood fall, he told me later. He seemed to like my company, and we danced a lot together.

They were there the following week, and again claimed quite a few dances. John asked if he could see me home, but I declined. I didn't want to put any obstacle in the way of a possible alliance with Henry. How blind I was.

Next Saturday again saw us at St. Mary's, but on the way home Grace said:

"I shan't see you tomorrow night Elsie, I've got a date. You don't mind do you?" I felt an ominous, sinking feeling.

"No – 'course not. Who is it? Tom?" – I wanted to know.

"Oh no – not him. He's alright to dance with, but I wouldn't go out with him. I'll – I'll tell you later." I shrugged. Why the mystery?

But what a shock I got on the Sunday night. Mam came back from an evening's drinking at the Derby Arms with Dad. The Derby Arms was across the road from where Grace lived.

"Ya'll never guess who I've seen," Mam said. She paused for emphasis. "With Grace," she added.

"I don't know Mam, who?" she paused again before she spoke.

"Grace and Henry Wilson."

"Grace and HENRY?" I echoed. "Oh but it can't be Mam. She she'd have told me. Besides – she's not his sort".

But suddenly my snug little world came tumbling around my ears. Oh – how COULD she – how COULD he? She knew how much I idolised him, how could she?

I cried in my pillow that night. I knew what they meant by a broken heart, and I never forgot that feeling of emptiness – for me the world had come to an end.

What a fool I was – what an idiot I had been all these years. The next day at the factory I didn't want to speak to anybody and when I passed Henry on the way to the toilets, he avoided my eyes and looked decidedly sheepish. But not half as sheepish as Grace looked.

And so next Saturday I went to St. Mary's on my own, and when John asked if he could see me home, I said 'yes', but without much enthusiasm. And of course he asked if he could see me the following evening, and if he could take me to the pictures in the week.

Grace didn't last long with Henry.

"He's too miserable," she told me. "Always looking on the black side of things. I told him, "Elsie would suit better.""

I looked at her askance, and even more so when she asked if we could continue our friendship.

Oh no - not this girl, I'd decided. Once bitten twice shy. Besides - I now had a boyfriend.

Chapter Fourteen

Courtship in the 1930s was a very serious affair. Once a boy and girl started 'going steady' it was accepted by all their friends and family that they would eventually marry.

Morals were much stricter then, it being considered by the majority that to anticipate marriage during courtship was sinful. What a prude I must have been at that time. But for all that there were plenty of 'shotgun weddings', 'forceputs', and some even got married in white when the girl's waistline was decidedly bulky; in the eyes of the Church a most sinful thing to do.

To me, straight-laced as I was, virginity was the greatest prize a man had a right to expect. Alas – today the reverse seems to be the accepted thing.

The Pill has made an undoubted change in todays morals. If the Pill had been introduced in the 1930s, would I have been so concerned about virginity, the purity of a bride? I wonder. As soon as it was established that I was 'going steady', I bought things for my 'bottom drawer', towels, pillow slips, and kitchen utensils. I was still not getting much of a wage in 1936, George Beardsley's being noted for their lack of co-operation in that respect. But – I was in full-time work.

One day Mam, who incidentally thought John a nice lad, said to me, "If ya' like Elsie ya' can start payin' board – now that yer' courtin'." Good old Mam! I hadn't dared broach the subject myself, always being a little afraid of her.

So – I now had a definite sum of money I could save every week. I was still not wildly elated at the prospect that I now had a young man. I still played lots of tennis, especially on Saturday afternoon, and was still very much aware of Henry.

But another boy had come on the scene. He lived near the Hospital, and would be leaning, apparently nonchalantly on the gate by Savage's farm each time I passed. He was tall and tanned, with a thick mane of tawny hair; a really likeable chap.

"Hallo - playing tennis again?" he asked.

So I stopped, and talked, and learned that he helped on the farm; was rather a loner and had a motor-bike and side car.

"Would it be alright if I came down to watch?"

"Yes of course." I was intrigued. I could see he was interested in me. Are they going to fall over each other, I wondered, now that I have a fella?

He was there the following week. Granville, as I will call him, to save embarrassment, though I must tell you that was not his real name, said he wished he could play too.

"You'll have to have some rubber plimsolls," I told him. "Then you can play next week."

There were a few raised eyebrows among the others, for it was obvious that he'd 'set his stall' at me, to use an Ilkeston slang expression, and they knew that I already had a young man.

But I was enjoying the situation. I'd always taken a back seat where romance was concerned. But although Granville was at the courts every week he never played tennis, because he always turned up wearing boots. He'd just sit there watching me.

I beginning to like him a lot, he was so handsome, so friendly, and I was fast approaching a state of indecision. What if he asked me to be his girl?

One day the inevitable happened. I'd taken my sister Marie with me. She was so shy, and always moping about the house on her own. Mam was getting concerned.

"I wish she'd find a pal," she said. "Why don't ya' tek her wi' you."

"Oh but Mam," I started, then relented. I was being selfish I suppose. "Oh - alright then. Come on."

And she really did enjoy that afternoon, although she only

sat and watched. But I expect she looked at me with a kind of hero worship, for wasn't I doing the kind of things she must have secretly, in her own withdrawn world, yearned for?

Granville was there. He'd even brought his motor cycle combination with him.

"I thought I could run you home," he told me. So Marie sat behind me in the side-car, and I felt very important being driven home by this handsome young man, but I was soon to be brought down to earth.

"What are you doing tonight?" he asked. "Would you like to go for a run out somewhere?" I felt trapped – and floundered.

"Er – I'm going to the pictures," I told him.

"Who with?" He looked surprised.

"My – my young man." I felt terrible.

"Young man? But why didn't you tell me before?"

So that was that. He took me home but never came to the Sports Ground again, although we never actually quarrelled. I felt pretty awful for a long time about that, but I suppose I was strictly a 'one man girl'. Another lesson I had learned in life.

Our courtship progressed steadily, and I was taken home one evening when it poured with rain to meet Our Dad. John's mother had died two years previously.

Home was a narrow terraced house with the back door opening into the entry between two houses. There was a sink with a cold water tap in one corner, and a 'lav' across an uneven brick yard.

John's Dad was a thin, stooped man with a moustache who forever talked about the Boer War, and the men who used assegais.

I was seated in a high backed arm chair, and felt like a little girl on trial. But I seemed to be approved of, and the old man told me to "Cum' agen' mi' gel."

Not many weeks after that John told me he'd had second thoughts about marriage. His father had always been a travelling man, 'travelled wi' the Gypsy folk', and had dealt in lino, pots and hardware, and had also sold horses.

Back Yard

When he was younger John had travelled around for a while with his father, and had grown to enjoy the life of bargaining and peddling. So it was no wonder that he'd wanted to follow in his father's footsteps. All at once he'd got a hankering to send for a crate of pots, and some remnants and hire himself a market stall. Obviously I wouldn't fit in - I'd be a hindrance, so, reluctantly he told me what he'd decided to do.

I was most upset as was Mam when I told her. I think the biggest blow was to my pride. So I had a good cry and felt better afterwards. But a few days later a very sheepish looking John was at our house, full of apologies.

He didn't know what had come over him to want to end our courtship, and he'd had a right ticking-off from his Dad.

"Ya' daft thing - fancy letting a nice gel' like that go". And so we kissed and made up, and decided to start again. But in later years he'd often talk about that crate of pots, and the golden opportunity he'd let slip away, and I'd say, "Well why not have a go now? Hire a market stall and I'll help you." But the venture never materialised. I think it must have been just another 'Flash in the pan'.

In the 1930s many girls went to the altar knowing little or nothing about sex and procreation, apart from what they'd learned in the school playground, or whispered among their friends at work.

There were no sex lessons at school as there are now, and periods were a very taboo subject. A few enlightened parents told their sons and daughters the facts of life, but they were very much in the minority. Some mothers would tell their daughters on starting courting,

"Now mind you behave yourself. We don't want any trouble here." No explanation of what this mysterious 'trouble' was. Mam sent out lots of veiled hints.

"Don't get standin' at bottom o' that entry too long. There's no bloody good in it." No wonder I was scared to death, and when one day she was going on about a girl who was reputed to be 'a bit easy', she said, "And look what her's got fer' not behavin' hersen'. A bun in th' oven."

So - was it any wonder that girls were scared to death to follow the call of nature, and that their prime objective was to keep themselves pure and virginal for the right man.

My, my - how things have changed.

Chapter Fifteen

1938, and I was really 'going steady', and a great affection was growing between us. Oh, John and I had our disagreements, but quickly made it up again. In the Summer we went long walks, and when it rained, went to the pictures.

Saturday evenings would see us in one of the local pubs. We hardly ever went out of town, except on rare occasions to the Empire at Nottingham, when we had to get a bus. There weren't so many cars owners then. Besides, we were saving for when we eventually got married.

Then there started to be threats of discontent coming from the Continent. Clouds of war seemed to be looming. A chap named Hitler was rounding up the pick of the German youths, the cream of the country and putting them in the Army. Apparently he had dreams of a Super race, that could vanquish everything in it's path.

"He's a mad bogger," declared our Dad.

"He'll not come to 'owt," our Mam assured him. "Them sort never do. All mouth and n'owt cummin' out."

We couldn't have cared less, we were too interested in preparing for our little nest.

But by June the rumblings of discontent grew worse, and a Nation-wide drive was planned to make Britain safe from air attack. Air Raid Wardens were introduced, just ordinary men who were good at leadership. The A.R.P. Air Raid Precaution was formed and soon lots of patriotic citizens rushed to join.

To many people it was all a bit of fun. Po-oh – there'd be no war. Wasn't the Great War, the 1914-1918 conflagration, the war to end all wars?

Nevertheless, I was caught up in the tide of patriotic fervour.

I joined the Red Cross First Aid classes held at Gladstone School. One or other of the local doctors would talk to us about wounds, fractures and bleeding. I'd listen entranced; the mysteries and functions of the human body had always fascinated me. When the doctor spoke of the several forms of bleeding, Capillary, from a trickle to little sharp spurts, and Arterial, gushing in large spurts, I noticed several men leave the room.

"Gone for a wee," I thought, until one man actually slumped to the floor.

"S'alright," the lecturer told us, "It's always the men who faint." I enjoyed the bandaging sessions, and learning about the various bones of the body.

Then I joined the A.R.P. proper, and had to learn about Aerial Warfare, and the various gasses. One day our section had to don gas-masks and enter a room beside the Town Hall, which was filled with tear-gas. This was to prove the effectiveness of the masks. When we took them off outside, the gas which had collected in our clothes made our eyes stream with tears. It was a most painful experience.

Another time we assembled on a piece of ground on Manners road, where the Swimming Baths now stand. A bonfire had been lit in a large, corrugated iron shed, a sack hung over each end opening, and we had to crawl around on all fours, to demonstrate the clarity of the air around the ground. Briefly we had to stand erect, but we choked so much we were glad to get back to floor level.

If war started, the enemy would drop incendiary bombs we were told. What other fiendish things would be in store, we wondered?

By 1939 Air Raid Shelters were being distributed; in cities at first, which were most vulnerable to air attack. Then people started digging huge holes in their gardens and building their own shelters. Talk about 'going to ground'.

The Home Guard was formed, an army of the people; patriotic, caring men who wouldn't give up their homes, their birthright without a heck of a fight. They were issued with khaki trousers, putees and tunics, and chip-bag caps, and drilled with all the fervour of a real army.

Sundays would see them out on manoeuvres, their rifles empty, but ready for any onslaught that came their way.

John would arrive home sweaty, with soil grimed face, but as elated as if he'd been in a real battle.

"I caught ten 'Jerries' today, in an ambush; came right on 'em from behind."

I'd listen to him, so proud, but hoping that it would never come to a real fight.

And so the Summer wore on, both of us caught up in our own patriotic fervour, me becoming an ambulance attendant, and John deep into the Home Guard manoeuvres. We just accepted that as British subjects we should do our duty as we thought best. Then in September Hitler and his army invaded Poland. Straight away came the complete mobilisation of our Army, Navy and Air Force, and all fit men between the ages of 18 and 40 were conscripted to serve their country.

Certain men in key positions were exempt; and of course there were the usual conscientious objectors, mostly objecting on religious grounds. John was a spare crane driver at Stanton – crane driver was classed in an exempted category, but he told me if he had to join up he would apply to go in the Navy, as a stoker, because he knew such a lot about boilers.

Mr. Neville Chamberlain, who was Prime Minister at that time, travelled to Munich to try to get a settlement to the crisis. Peace at any price was what he aimed for. The talks had apparently gone well, and a smiling Mr. Chamberlain was shown on all our cinema screens, waving that vital piece of paper in the air.

Alas, this triumph was short-lived, and on September 3rd 1939 we were at war with Germany.

Black-out restrictions were introduced, and hundreds of yards of black material were hurriedly sewn to kill the light of gas and electric from houses and business premises. Broad, sticky tape was criss-crossed over window panes to cut out the risk of flying glass during a possible air raid.

Car headlights were shaded, as were the street lamps, and people found their way about with the aid of a hand torch.

Gas masks were issued, and everybody was advised to carry them about at all times. They were contained in an oblong tin with straps of webbing threaded through, so that they could be carried over our shoulders.

Oh it was a really gloomy prospect, but as is usual when the British are up against it we made light of the situationn and a real comradeship sprang up between people who had been sworn enemies for years. Old feuds were quickly forgotten.

An advert appeared in our local 'rag', 'Down with Hitler' – up with Beer – come to the Victoria and be of good cheer', which well illustrates the good spirit of the people of Britain.

The bombing of Britain began, and at the factory the first topic of conversation each morning would be the War situation.

"Did y'hear th' news on wireless last night? It's gerrin' bad 'int it?" We were all united in our fear.

"I've got a bag packed ready," another woman informed us, "Wi' some clean clothes in, an' some fags an' mi' bank book, in case we get bombed." We were incredulous. "But what happens if ya' get bombed out while ye'r at work?" We wanted to know.

"Oh well" – she shrugged, "I allus' carry a spare pair o' bloomers in mi' 'andbag – in case mi' others gets wet."

Cheerful? That's what kept us all going.

The air raid sirens often sounded during the night, especially if enemy bombers were detected coming over the Derbyshire area. Stanton Ironworks on the outskirts of Ilkeston was, of course, a prime target, although the only bombs ever dropped there fell in a field outside the works, as did an enemy plane.

When the siren wailed it's warning I'd dress in navy slacks, a woollen jumper and dark mac. Of course, it was pitch black everywhere, with all the lights being shrouded, or dimmed altogether, and I had a quarter of a mile to walk to the First Aid Post at Bennerley School.

As a weapon, in case of a possible attack on my person, I'd carry a large, heavy iron poker, but wrapped in a newspaper, to defend myself. This raised some laughter, I can tell you. Mam used to come downstairs and sit in the pantry until the All Clear went. Dad would usually be down the pit, and Dan and the two younger children would be fast asleep upstairs.

One night, about three in the morning after the All Clear had sounded, I came home, my eyes crying out for sleep. Mam was distinctly peeved about something.

"Ya' want to think about us a bit more - dashin' off there as soon as 'siren goes," she told me.

So - I ignored the call to duty for a while, but felt rather bitter about it.

Then a man who lived next door, a rather timid, much frightened man started knocking us up and seeking shelter when the sirens had sounded. He and his wife and our Mam would sit on the pantry steps, talking and shaking until the All Clear had sounded.

One day he brought a crate full of beer bottles, and asked if he could put them on the 'thrall' down the pantry.

"Then we shall be sure of a drink." Mam was all for it. But one night the sirens had sounded, and Mam still slept on.

"Mam - sirens has' gone," I called.

"Oh bugger the bombs," she answered sleepily. "I'll die in mi' bed if I has to."

But a repeated thumping came on the back door - under our bedroom window.

"Who is it?" I called angrily as I drew up the sash window.

"It's me - it's Wilf. Let us in - there's an air raid."

"Oh - go back to bed," I shouted, then, greatly daring. "Why don't y'act more like a man," and I banged the window shut.

But first thing next morning he was at our back door to fetch back his crate of beer bottles.

Chapter Sixteen

1939 dragged on into 1940. The bombs were coming thick and fast - tons of them over the big cities, London, Coventry, Birmingham. We'd listen to the news with despair in our hearts, and pray for the poor souls who had lost their homes and loved ones.

Children were evacuated to the country, to safer places, and a few found their way to Ilkeston.

Rationing was introduced. Meat, bread, sweets and clothes could only be bought with coupons from our Ration Books. Quite naturally there was soon a Black Market in these items, a lot of subdued talk. 'Could ya' do wi' an extra bit o' bacon?' 'Ah' know someone who has sum' clothin' coupons ta' sell'. And so it went on.

Gas masks were issued, horrible, smelly, rubber things in a tin box. I felt sick the first time I donned mine. We had to carry the offending tins with us wherever we went. Nobody would dream of going anywhere without their tin box.

"We look a right lot o' buggers in these," our Mam said, when she first tried hers on.

Appeals were being sent out by Womens' organisations for blankets knitted with wool remnants, and for socks and Balaclava helmets for our fighting men. Mam started to knit squares of different coloured wools, and made a huge blanket. All her energies were channelled into this War effort of hers. When it was finished she handed it into a Central collecting station, a Chapel schoolroom, and when a letter came from headquarters thanking her for her most welcome contribution she was as 'chuffed' as if she'd been awarded the OBE.

She no longer grumbled when I went to the first Aid Post,

having now, herself, been bitten with the bug of patriotism.

Once a week I was on all night duty - usually Saturday nights. I'd take tea and milk, rashers of bacon and a few sausages, and fry them in the school staff room next morning. Sylvia Merry, a chemist's daughter, who was always on duty with me, would bring bread and a tin of tomatoes and we'd have a good old 'fry up'.

We slept on fold-up beds on a classroom floor, and it was really eerie to wake up in that strange place. We took it in turns to sleep, there being six or more on duty. A billiard table had been loaned for the men, but we girls had found a basket full of costume items, crinolines, stoles, large hats, fans etc., for use in school amateur dramatics. We spent some hilarious hours dressing up in these clothes, and making up one act plays.

Of course there were the odd little 'affairs' on the side; unavoidable I suppose when men and young women are thrown together. I, being so straight-laced, was quite shocked at these goings on, but the others merely shrugged.

"It'll all end when war finishes."

We often went out on night manoeuvres, bumping along in the black out in our make shift ambulance, gas-masks and First Aid Kits at the readyn and finishing up at the most unlikely spots - often among farm buildings.

There'd be 'bodies' scattered about, with blood on their head and arms, and with printed tags on their jackets - 'bone protruding through right sleeve,' 'Eyes glazed,' 'Breathing shallow,' 'A state of shock'.

I liked the ones best which said 'broken femur, foot hanging sideways.' because this was my favourite bandaging accomplishment.

Sometimes a notice would tell us 'A smell of rotten eggs,' 'Smell of marsh gas,' etc. and then we'd have to don our gas masks.

Oh - we were all in deadly earnest I can assure you, and confident we'd have made a good account of ourselves had we been put to the test.

Life went on much as in peace time; people got married, but there was a lot of borrowing and lending of wedding finery. Furniture too was bought with units, a form of rationing. When the shops had sold out of all their good, pre-war furniture, Utility furniture was introduced. This was plain, cheap, stained wood which just fulfilled the purpose for which it was intended. It was horrible, unattractive stuff. No wonder it was called Utility.

Wedding receptions were cut down to a bare minimum, guests and family alike all pooling their food coupons.

That dark Winter of 1940 gave way to the first warm days of Spring, and it was my birthday. I was twenty eight, and still not married. John still had not been 'called up' although many of his mates were now on active service.

March 16th, my birthday was clear and bright, and I was surprised when John called for me during the afternoon.

"We're going up-town," he told me. I was curious until we eventually stopped outside a jeweller's shop.

"Rings?" I asked. He nodded, grinning all over his face.

"Yes – engagement rings. I thought we might as well get engaged seeing as how it's your birthday."

So – we chose the ring, and my eyes were as bright as the diamonds set in a little cluster.

We went to the pictures first house, then down to the Popular, where I celebrated with a port.

"You can have the best drink in the house," he told me.

We were very happy that day, the War far from our minds, except for the black-out, as he walked me the mile and a half home.

My cousin Gladys from Nottingham announced that she was getting married, and would I be her bridesmaid? She agreed that a long, pale blue silk dress with short, puffed sleeves, one I'd worn for dancing would be ideal, and, with a bandeau of artificial flowers for my hair, a great saving for both of us.

The wedding was at Wollaton Church, Gladys looked tall and elegant in a close fitting dress of ivory satin, long tight sleeves and the dress gently flaring from the waist. It was simple and beautiful. The small reception was at Ron's, the bridegroom's home, and afterwards, Gladys and Ron set off on his motorbike for their brief honeymoon.

But whilst we were dressing at Aunt Ethel's house, before the wedding Gladys said.

"Why not try this dress on Elsie? Then if it fits you you can borrow it for your wedding."

Chapter Seventeen

The Spring of 1940 was a happy time for me, for wasn't I now engaged to be married?

Happy that is except for the War situation. The sirens sounded almost every night, and the newspapers next morning carried horrendous accounts of the bombing and burning of our cities, and of the deliverance from this nightmare.

Factory life went on as usual, and I was given plenty of good advice from the girls now that I was engaged, most about the sexual side of marriage. I tried to appear as though I knew it all, but I listened avidly to them all the same.

We still played tennis, mostly on Saturday afternoons, and the clear blue skies and fresh air and laughter, and friendliness made one almost forget we were at warm

But the removal of iron railings from our park, and from the fronts of private houses, to be used in munitions brought the reality back to us with a shock. And now, forty years later the Park is still unenclosed, a grim reminder of the War Years.

And then suddenly, one day in June John said to me,

"Let's get married Else, shall we?"

"But where shall we live?"

"Why at our house of course. Where'd ya think?"

At that time there were some pairs of semi-detached houses being built by the Hospital, £350 each. Yes, I know, unbelievable isn't it? I'd been looking at them longingly for months. They were in a wonderful position, and with open fields at the back.

"Can't we buy one of those new ones, up Heanor Road? We could get a mortgage; I could keep on at work."

"But what if I get called up, and - 'owt happens. What

would we do then? Else – I'd like to, but we darsn't – not just now."

So, it was agreed that we live at his Dad's, on Slade Street. I wasn't very enchanted with the idea at first, it was such a dark, poky little house. But the main thing was, we'd be married, I'd have my man by my side.

Slade Street

Then all at once I began to have doubts. Marriage was such a final, irrecoverable step. What it we didn't get on?

"Yer' never know till yer've lived together a bit," someone told me. "First ten years ar't the worst" another said.

I really had the 'colly-wobbles' bad, but kept it to myself. We planned to get married on August 3rd, and went to see the Vicar, Harry Price, at Cotmanhay Church.

I wrote to Cousin Gladys who now lived at Coventry, asking for the loan of her wedding dress. A sister of John's said I could borrow her veil, so I only had a hair bandeau of orange blossom to buy; I already had white satin dance shoes which would just peep from under my long dress.

Talk about a Utility wedding.

We couldn't have a big reception because of the food rationing, so we planned for just the immediate wedding group, best man, and one bridesmaid, and Mam and Dad and the kids.

Of course we had to ask my two Aunties from Nottingham, Aunt Ethel and Aunt Minnie, so naturally they'd stop for tea. There'd be about fourteen altogether. The rest of John's family were to be asked round later for wine, and wedding cake. What a difference to today's lavish receptions costing hundreds of pounds.

We wouldn't be having a honeymoon. Coastal areas, popular seaside places were definitely out with enemy planes often jettisoning their bombs on their way back to Germany. No – we'd just have to stay at home – have a honeymoon when the War was finished.

So – we made our plans, we bought the ring – I had my wedding finery ready, and John decorated the large front bedroom where he lived, with pink distemper. We now call it emulsion paint. We pooled what money we had left and bought a lovely mahogany bedroom suite, one the shop had in stock before the advent of Utility furniture. We also bought an oak dining suite, and a Ewbank washer, (the old, wallow a stick round type), on the never-never, for we'd now run out of money. Not a penny left between us, after we'd paid for my sheaf of lillies, and white carnations for the men.

But we were full of hope, although I was still having nightmares when I went to bed. What a timid, frightened creature I must have been.

The War still raged on, but we were now all more hopeful for we had a new Prime Minister, Mr. Winston Churchill, a tough, no nonsense man with a bull-dog tenacity. Wherever he went he cheered up the British people with his two fingers formed into a Victory sign.

What a terribly traumatic time to be leader of a nation.

My friends at the First Aid Post, the men as well as the women said they'd be forming a Guard of Honour outside the Church, so I bought a bottle of sherry and some biscuits for them to celebrate with at the Post.

I still wasn't too happy at the thought of starting married life in a poky, little terraced house, and if I'd known then that we'd be stuck there for the next fifteen years before moving to a better house, I think I'd have changed my mind about getting married.

Slowly the Wedding Day drew nearer, and I was still having bouts of panic. And then suddenly it all vanished, and when August 3rd dawned bright and sunny, with a cloudless sky, I knew everything would be alright.

The furniture had been delivered to 14 Slade St, as had all my bottom drawer utensils. The ham and tongue sandwiches were cut ready, and covered with a damp tea-towel. The port and sherry were put on a cupboard in the parlour, and the one tier wedding cake was delivered.

The long sheaf of lillies was brought after dinner time, and the men's buttonholes; John and the best man's being taken to the bridegroom's house.

The wedding was to be at 3 o'clock. Then at 10 o'clock I started having the 'runs'. I'd never be strong enough to stand at the altar I was sure.

"Better 'ave some nutmeg an' milk," Mam told me. "What ya' got to worry about? Yer'll be alright."

But at 2 o'clock she begged a drop of brandy from next door. That seemed to do the trick, and in a slight haze I was able to finish dressing.

Dad had his best suit on, and looked very smart with his trilby hat set at a jaunty angle. Mam was wearing a blue, flowered dress I'd made for her, and a new straw hat.

My bridesmaid, Vera, looked lovely in my long, turquoise dance dress, and with a small cluster of flowers perched over her forehead, and a posy to carry.

I took a long look at myself in the over-mantle mirror, and decided I looked the perfect bride, demure, virginal, but with stars in my eyes, and I decided at that moment that I'd live up to my marriage vows, and be a true and faithful wife.

Then the hired car arrived and Dad asked,

"Art'a ready mi' gel?"

The day was scorching hot and the scent of lillies almost overpowering in the confines of the car.

Then we were at the church and walking towards the altar, and the bridegroom and his best man. I turned to pass my bouquet to my bridesmaid, and saw Mam smiling at me, and there were unaccustomed tears in her eyes, and I felt a great rush of affection for her.

And then the Vicar was speaking in those strong, slow tones,

"Wilt thou John .... Wilt thou Elsie?" and I tried to imprint every word on my mind, so that I'd remember them all my married life. And I vowed again that I'd be a good wife, and mother too when the time came.

Christ Church, Cotmanhay